THE HILL

By
Lamont Carey

Edited by

Rashidah Denton
Miranda Manning
Christian Graham
Salana Tyson
Melanee Woodard

**Book Design and graphics
Created by**

Leslie "Chuck" McLeod, President, Rap Ent.

Photo of Lamont Carey taken by
April Sims Photography

LaCarey Entertainment, LLC
www.lacareyentertainment.com
"Success Is My Only Option"

ISBN: 978-0-9816200-3-9

1

THE HILL

Copyright © 2011 by Lamont Carey

Distributed Worldwide

Special Thanks

Special thanks to Pharaoh, Libra, Geraldine Carey, Tracy Carey, Pat Carey, Jermain Ingram, Adar Ayira, Robert Garrett, Melanee Woodard, Kevin Pendergrass, Helen Williams, Miranda Manning, Christine Graham, Salana T, Leslie "Chuck" Mcloud, Chucky May, Doc Powell, DRE', Tbrooks, James "Ping" Cook, Marc Weathers, Melanie Washington, Alqamar, Rashidah Denton, Mary Brown, Life Pieces To Master Pieces, Kevin Hicks, Joe Briggs, Karen Jones, Joy Marshall, Pam Baker, Afi, The Laws Of The Street Cast, Manny, Allie Bird, Lakeisha Washington,Tinyman, John Blunt, Rev. Steward III, Chosen, Bro. Rob, Andrea Camille, Tom Brown, Wesui, Mark Thompson, Kimoni, Brenda Richardson, Monday Childs, Jennifer Sweat, Robert Robertson,Tracy Wiggs, Matthew Lorie, Cedric Henderson, Dennis Sobin, Dana, Tony Johnson, GLAM, INC, April Sims, Tammy Brown, Bianca Brown, Gayle Johnson, Joy Washington, Brook G, Jane, My First Love family, my social network family, my fans, and any and everyone I forgot.

R.I.P
GG
Will Da Real One

Dear Readers:

I wrote this book while in prison. It took me close to a decade to release it because I was exploring other creative ventures. My reason for writing this is to remind you that we all make mistakes. Learning and growing from those mistakes should be the focus.

This book insert is also for the current prisoner or ex-offender who is struggling to figure out how to move on with their lives in a productive manner. I know it seems grim because now you have convictions which are another barrier in your ability to change your life for the better. However, I am an example that it can be done. There are still no limitations to what you can accomplish now or after your release.

One of the things I did was repackage my past and made it a positive force for my future. This simply means taking what you already know and using it to benefit you in a positive way. You can decide to become a speaker in an effort to prevent youth from following in your footsteps. You can get involved with the changing of laws that effect prisoners and ex-offenders. You can address issues that you are passionate about through the arts. I wrote six books, seven screenplays, and three children books while in prison. I then came home and started directing plays at places like the John F. Kennedy Center and shooting independent film projects that you will learn more about at the back of the book. I even started several companies, did a few speaking tours as well as spokenword performances. I am no different than you are. Actually, you may be in a better position to succeed than I had.

See, I grew up in public housing with parents who had their own issues. I went to prison as a juvenile so I didn't graduate from school.

I did a total of eleven years in prison. I came home with no real marketable skills. Statistics would suggest that I am and would be a failure and repeat offender for the rest of my life. However I didn't and don't share that belief. Instead I excel just like you will. See, the sky is not the limit. You can soar as high as you can dream and you can accomplish whatever it is your heart desires.

The first step is to believe that you will be successful. Then believe you will make it happen. Start by writing down what it is that you want to do and figure out all of the ways you can accomplish it. Then follow those steps. If you are in prison, you can still start there. You don't have to wait until you are free to live. Live and thrive now.

In closing, THE HILL was an idea. I turned it into a book. The dream was for you to read it! Dream accomplished.

Lamont Carey

Chapter One

The fearful eyes of sixty inmates dressed in orange prison jumpsuits peered through the bars that covered the windows of the bus. As it drove along the massive prison compound known as Lorton, the bus stopped at the first of two closed gate entrances to the Occoquan maximum security prison. They could see Sergeant Ruckus staring down at the bus from the upper level open doorway of the guard tower. He held an M-16 at the ready.

A deathly silence consumed the bus. Hearts started to rapidly pound. Their eyes remained locked on Sergeant Ruckus. He was a sure sign that they have just entered hell. He slowly walked over to the railing of the tower with his assault rifle firmly in hand as he peered down at the bus.

Corporal Bird walked out the exit door of the tower. He held a long black pole with a mirror connected to its end. He stood and stared at the bus. Ruckus then signaled to someone inside the tower. Seconds later, the first gate screeched as it slowly opened. The bus drove up to the second security gate and stopped. The first gate closed behind the bus.

Corporal Bird was buzzed through a side door that was built into the gate. He walked over to the bus and began to scan underneath of the bus with his instrument. After he circled the bus, he nodded his approval to Ruckus. The second gate screeched open and the bus drove a mile to the building where all new inmates are processed.

The building stretched a half of a block with a long walkway that seemed to disappear between a narrow pathway which led to the entrance doors. From a distance it looked like two buildings. There were at least fifty prisoners that lounged around on both sides of the walkway. They all wore the prison uniform of blue cotton slacks, blue button down shirts, and black boots. They watched the bus as the door opened. U.S. Marshall Jackson made his way off the bus.

"Move back!"

He barked at the prisoners who were hanging around the entrance. They nonchalantly strolled along the walkway, where the new arrivals must travel to enter inside the prison. The inmates positioned themselves in a way that provided a view of the bus. Some were hoping to see someone they knew. Some were looking for prey. The rest just wanted to see the new prisoners.

Jackson walked back onto the prison bus and peered at the inmates seated behind the metal gate that separates them from himself and the driver. Everyone looked at the Marshall, some in fear. Others displayed impatience. The remainder simply awaited Jackson's directions.

"When you exit the bus, ALL of you will walk down that long walkway! You will be met by a prison guard at the end of the walk. During this walk, you may see somebody you know. But, you better not stop! Once you get to the guard, he or she will tell you what's expected of you. So, now I want the right row to come off the bus first. Starting with the two men in the front then I want the left row to do the same. Let's move!!" shouted Jackson

7

The inmates who sat on the right side of the bus all stood up, shackled and handcuffed. The handcuffs were locked to a waist chain. Jackson unlocked and opened the metal gate that separated them from the officers. Then he stepped off the bus.

The driver told them to get off the bus. The men filed out one by one. Some were carrying clear bags that contained all of their belongings. Sherman was the last man to exit the bus. He was a medium build twenty four year old with a sandy brown complexion. He had no facial hair.

Sherman tried to stretch but being chained up made it difficult. He then took a deep breath and blew it out towards the hot air.

"Down the walkway!" Jackson yelled out.

The Marshall pointed toward the walkway. Sherman looked at the Marshall then started walking. He looked at the prisoners as he continued to walk down the walkway. Some of the inmates had smiles on their faces, others frowned at him. The rest were expressionless. The ages of the men appeared to vary from as old as sixty and as young as sixteen. Sherman thought he saw someone he knew from the streets but when he looked again, it didn't look like the guy.

The big red brick building surrounded the walkway. Once Sherman reached the middle of the walkway, Howard and Tim blocked his path. Tim put his hand on Sherman's chest.

Howard was a tall, light skinned man with a muscular build. Tim was black as the night sky without the moon. He was shorter than Howard with a solid build.

8

Tim stared sinisterly at him. Sherman stared back, unintimidated.

"Slim, what's up?! What the fuck you doing?" asked Sherman.

"Bitch, shut up! I want those tennis shoes!" said Tim.

"Nigga, you better get the fuck out of my way!" Sherman sneered.

Tim looked at his friend. Howard then reached into his pants and pulled out a seven inch jail knife. Tim stared back into Sherman's eyes.

"Either I'm going to get those shoes from a walking man," said Tim, "or a dead man. Your choice."

Sherman was mad, but he knew the man would kill him. He glanced around and saw three other inmates being robbed of their shoes as well.

Sherman didn't resist as Tim knelt to remove Sherman's Air Jordan tennis shoes, Both inmates then walked off without saying another word to Sherman. Sherman walked to the entrance where the prison guard stood. The guard stopped him at the door and pointed to Sherman's feet.

"Where are your tennis shoes? Why do you only have on socks?" asked Corporal Stevenson.

"I didn't wear any tennis shoes down here," answered Sherman.

"You're a damn lie!" Corporal Stevenson shouted. "Follow me!"

Sherman followed Stevenson down a long hallway. Prisoners passed by laughing and pointing at Sherman's feet. The floors of the long hallway were dark brown. The walls were painted a dingy light brown. Stevenson stopped at a closed metal door and knocked on it. There was a voice on the other side of the door that yelled, "Come in!" Stevenson opened the door and waved Sherman into the room. He walked into the small room. A large wooden desk stacked with piles of files and papers covered the entire desk. Major Brazil, a huge white man with short blond hair, sat towering over the desk. He appeared trapped between his desk and two long metal cabinets on each side of him. The Major looked at the two men who just entered his office.

"How may I help you, gentlemen?" asked the Major.

"Major Brazil, this new arrival had his tennis shoes taken," said Corporal Stevenson.

"Man, I didn't wear no damn tennis shoes down here!" exclaimed Sherman.

The huge man stood and walked over to Sherman.

"I don't have time for your bullshit. If you want to be a tough guy, this is the place to be it. There are plenty of killers here waiting on guys like you to get pregnant. Now you have one or two options. Option one, tell me who took your shoes. Option two, find them yourself," said the Major.

"Man, I didn't have any damn shoes." Sherman barked.

The Major nodded his head, "Corporal, I want you to take him down to the property room and get him some *boots. Have them fit him for a body bag, too. He won't last long here. Then I want you to check his bad ass in."*

"What?" asked Sherman, "Why in the fuck you putting me in protective custody! I ain't scared of no fucking body. I came here with no shoes on!"

The Major stepped so close to Sherman's face that his nose almost touched his.

"Listen here. I don't know where you learnt your manners, but this is my house. You want to show your ass here, we will beat that ass here. You can't be too bad, your shoes were taken off of your feet and you just got off the bus. So I am going to offer you a little advice that you should take to heart. Adjust your attitude. I didn't do shit to get you here, but as long as you're here, you will respect me or fear me. Now I am going to give you a chance to cool off in the hole. After we investigate whether or not you came with shoes or you wore the same size as someone else, we may allow you on the compound. But for now your ass is going on lockdown. Good day, Sir," said the Major.

"Motherfucker! I'm not going on PC!" shouted Sherman.

"Corporal Stevenson, get him out of here. First I want him processed, and then he goes to the property room."

"Yes sir," answered Stevenson.

Sherman knew there was nothing he could say or do to stop him from going on administration, so he didn't protest.

11

Stevenson turned to Sherman, "Follow me."

Stevenson turned and walked out of the Major's office with Sherman following him. Sherman angrily mumbled to himself all the way down the hall. Tim was leaning against the wall. He had Sherman's tennis shoes on his feet, engaging in conversation with two other prisoners. When he spotted Sherman and Stevenson, he just stared into Sherman's eyes. The two men he was talking to continued to talk. They had no knowledge of Tim taking Sherman's shoes.

Sherman followed Stevenson into the property room. He noticed the men who were on the bus with him locked behind a large holding cell on the far left side of the room. They were now dressed in the institution's outfits. His eyes wandered over the long wooden table in the middle of the room. Sergeant Hag was seated on the edge of the table, talking to another colleague who was not visible from the windowless cut in the wall. The hole was the size of a storefront window. The slot was near the holding cell.

Hag stood and took a ring of keys off his belt. He walked over to Sherman and unhooked the handcuffs from the waist chain. He then pulled the chain from around Sherman's waist allowing it to drop on the floor. After Hag unlocked the handcuffs, Sherman stretched his arms into the air. Hag knelt down to Sherman's feet and took off the shackles. Sherman started lifting his legs.

Hag looked Sherman in his eyes, "Strip! I want all of your clothes off."

Sherman looked at Buttacup, a white homosexual prisoner who suddenly appeared from the back area. Buttacup had on extremely tight-fitting pants and his eyebrows arched. He started sweeping the floor in the direction of the table.

Sherman looked back at the guard. "Where do I take them off at, in the shower?" he said, gesturing to the two shower stalls to his right.

"No, right here!" Hag barked.

Sherman looked over to the holding cell where the other inmates were. Some of the inmates were looking in the direction of Sherman and the guards. Sherman looked back at Buttacup. Buttacup's eyes quickly refocused from Sherman to the floor and he continued to sweep.

Sherman looked at Sergeant Hag, "Man, all these motherfuckers looking at me!"

"You don't have nothing we all don't already have," Hag barked.

Sherman didn't say anything else. He took all his clothes off, piece by piece, and handed them to Hag. Hag checked the clothes before tossing them on the table. Once Sherman had all of his clothes off, he stood in front of the officer in the nude. Sherman turned his head and caught Buttacup watching him. The homosexual quickly looked at the floor.

Hag noticed Buttacup's movement, "Buttacup! Go clean the showers!"

Buttacup turned and walked away.

The guard who was behind the metal cage started talking, "Hurry up with him! I'm trying to take my break."

Hag looked back at the cage window, "R-right."

Then he looked back at Sherman, "Squat, lift your nuts, and cough."

Sherman did what he was told and then stood up. Hag walked over to retrieve a pile of clothes from the guard on the other side of the wall. He handed Sherman a pair of cotton blue slacks, a blue shirt, and underclothes. Sherman put the clothes on.

Hag spoke, "Pick up your clothes and carry them over there," as he gestured toward the guard hidden from view.

Sherman walked over to the table, picked up his clothes and took them to the window. After handing the items over, the guard examined the clothes and wrote each item on a piece of paper. He handed the paper to Sherman. Sherman signed it and handed it back. The guard pulled a yellow page from the paper Sherman signed. The guard kept the original piece and handed the yellow copy to Sherman.

"Stay right here," said the guard, "so I can give you a roll and some extra clothes."

The guard left the window. Sherman peeked through the window and saw about ten racks full of clothes on hangers. There also was a small metal desk behind the window. A dark-skinned inmate with a bald head was sitting behind the desk typing. The inmate looked up and greeted Sherman with a nod. Sherman nodded back. The inmate then returned to typing. The guard came back to the window and handed Sherman a blanket roll. Inside of the blanket was two sheets, washcloths, a cup, pillowcase, a bar of soap and a toothbrush.

The guard also handed him a change of clothes, two pairs of underwear, and a pillow.

"That's all," said the guard from behind the window.

"Let's go," said Stevenson, as he walked over to Sherman.

The guard in the cage spoke, "Hold up, I forgot the boots."

The guard left the window again, and returned with a pair of boots. Sherman put the boots on, and then followed Stevenson back into the hallway. Other prisoners were still walking around the hall.

Sunlight beamed into the building as Stevenson opened a door leading to the outside. The guard signaled Sherman to follow him. They walked across the compound where there were eight small gray buildings resembling one level apartment buildings. The windows were small with screens fitted over them. Amongst the concrete walkways were patches of green grass.

About half a mile away, Sherman could see bleachers with about thirteen rows on a huge football field. Enclosing the field was a track. Inmates were playing football, jogging, or walking on the track, sitting or standing on the bleachers. Approximately five hundred inmates were on the field as the sun beamed down on them.

Sherman spotted four towers about a city block apart with two guards on each. One of the guards had a pair of binoculars for up-close surveillance. The second guard kept a pump shotgun in hand. Both monitored the actions of the inmates at all times. Sherman followed Stevenson into one of the small buildings as three of the other officers were exiting it. Once inside of the building, it was very quiet. The walls were of a light tannish color while the floor was dark brown. Sherman followed Stevenson over to the guard booth that was shaped like a spaceship. Fiber glass windows surround the booth. It was known as "The Bubble".

Three guards were positioned inside of The Bubble; Lieutenant Cooper, Officer Washington, and Officer Bacschew. Inside The Bubble was a control desk with about one hundred different switches and television monitors. Officer Bacshew walked to the door and opened it.

"What's up, Stevenson?"

Stevenson replied, "Nothing much. I have a newcomer for you. He is to be held until the conclusion of his pending investigation."

"What's up? What happened?" said Officer Bacshew.

Officer Washington steps out of the booth and looks down at the institutional boots Sherman's had on. "Somebody got him for his shoes."

"Nigga, I told you I didn't have any shoes! What the fuck you talking about somebody hit me for my shoes!? Ain't no motherfucker taking shit from me!" said Sherman.

Lieutenant Cooper came out of the booth and spoke, "Okay, my Friend. There is no need to get uptight. So, how much time do you have?"

"Five to fifteen years," Sherman answered.

"That's not bad compared to some of the others in here," Lieutenant Cooper replied.

"Nobody else concerns me." Sherman boasted.

"Okay sir," Lieutenant Cooper turned to Stevenson, "Thank you Corporal. I got it from here."

Stevenson and the Lieutenant shook hands. the Corporal left.

Lieutenant Cooper turned to Sherman, "Just follow me."

A white female officer came out of the booth. She had short blonde hair with a medium build. Her eyes were seawater blue. She had on very little make-up. She was also a Corporal.

The female Corporal asked, "Would you like for me to open a door?"

"Yes, hit forty-eight," said Cooper.

"Yes sir," said the female Corporal.

The woman walked back into the booth.

Cooper turned back to Sherman, "Follow me."

Sherman followed Cooper to a metal door that led to one of the prison's lockdown units. Silence broke as Cooper opened the door. The long hallway

*was dimly lit with about fifteen doors on each side.
Sherman continued to follow the officer. The inmates
on lockdown were banging, talking, singing, and
shouting from inside their cells. They weren't visible
from behind the metal gray doors. Two closed slots
were positioned on each door. The inmates continued
yelling, screaming and banging on the doors.*

"Quiet down in here!!" yelled Cooper.

A few of the inmates yelled back, "Fuck
You!!!," as they continued to make noise.

One inmate called the guard, "Hey Lieutenant!! Hey,
Lieutenant!!"

"What!?"

*Cooper walked to the inmate's door. The
guard did not open the slot.*

"What!" Cooper repeated.

"Open the motherfucking slot!!!"

"No! What do you want!?" Cooper said, smiling.

"Open the motherfucking slot, bitch nigga!!! I want
some ass!! Ha, ha, ha!!" laughed the inmate.

"Fuck you!!" Cooper replied.

"Nah! Lieutenant! Fo' real, Lieutenant! I want to
talk to you!!"

"I'm listening." Cooper replied.

"When do I come off lockdown!?"

"Who is that!" Cooper questioned.

"Daryl Robinson!!"

"Robinson, you come off tomorrow morning!," The Lieutenant replied.

"Yea. R-right! Fuck you then!!"

Sherman smiled and continued to follow Lieutenant Cooper. The inmates continued to make noise. The guard stopped in front of an open door. Above the door was the number forty-eight.

"This is your cell," Cooper told Sherman.

Sherman walked into the cell. The guard shut the door once Sherman was inside.

Chapter Two

*The white female officer opened the door.
Sherman walked into the big room. The first thing he
noticed was blue carpet. There was a long wooden
table in the room. Three people sat around the table.
There was a white woman in her mid forties. She had
red hair and wore small-framed glasses. She had a
medium build and wore a red silk blouse. Her pants
could not be seen because she was sitting in a chair
behind the table. There was also a white male in his
mid forties. His hair was crystal white. He was
neatly shaven and also wore small-framed glasses.
The man was of medium build and wore a white
short-sleeved shirt. He had two metal gold bars on
his shirt-sleeve that identified him as a Captain. He
sat to the right of the white woman. To her left, there
was a black male in his late thirties. He had
sprinkles of gray in his hair and his mustache. The
black man had a thin build and wore a dark blue suit
jacket, white shirt and a dark blue silk tie.*

*Once Sherman was inside the room, he
stood near the door. The Captain stood up and
motioned with his hand telling Sherman to come here.
The Captain pointed to one of the two chairs on the
opposite side of the table.*

"Please come in and have a seat."

*Sherman walked over to the table and sat
down in the chair to his right. He glanced around the
room. He saw a bookshelf with typewriters on it.
Then he looked directly at the white woman. Her
green eyes were shining like marbles. She smiled at
him, and then she extended her hand out to him.*

"How are you doing, Mr. Ford? My name is Mrs. Kelly. I will be your counselor while you're here at this facility."

Sherman shook the woman's hand. Then they both leaned back in their chairs.

The woman looked to her right. *"This is Captain Lok. He will be listening in on your classification hearing."*

The Captain just nodded his head at Sherman. Sherman glanced over at the captain. Then he looked back at Mrs. Kelly. Mrs. Kelly looked to her left.

"Mr. Ford, you have been here now for two weeks. Unfortunately, you ran into a few problems in the beginning. Mr. Ford, we have notified the District jail and they informed us that you had a pair of Air Jordan tennis shoes on before you left their custody. Now, what we do not know is what happened to those tennis shoes."

"I left them on the bus," said Sherman.

"Okay, well, we will be moving right along then."

Mrs. Kelly opened a folder that was in front of her.

"Mr. Ford, this is your file. On April 10, 1994, you were sentenced to serve five to fifteen years in this institution by Judge Mayhem, for carrying a firearm without a permit. Mr. Ford, you will go up for parole in seven months. Do you have a high school diploma?" Mrs. Kelly questioned.

"Yea." Sherman replied.

Would you like to get a trade while you're here?"
She asked him.

"Depends on what kind." Sherman nonchalantly
replied.

"We have plumbing, electricity, auto mechanics, meat
cutting and a welder shop. Do any of these interest
you?"

"Yea, the welder shop." Sherman stated.

"Okay, I will add your name to the waiting list. Do
you wish to stay in the lockdown unit or would you
like to go into population?" she inquired.

"I never wanted to be in the lockdown unit in the first
place."

"Well, you will come off today. Captain, which unit
will he be going to?" she asked.

The Captain ran his finger down a piece of paper he
had in front of him, "Housing unit three, five dorm,
and bunk thirteen."

"Can you remember that?" asked Mrs. Kelly.

"Yea, Unit three, five dorm, bunk thirteen. So, when
do I go?"

"You will be going as soon as you pack up," said the
Captain.

"So, is this all?" Sherman replied.

"Yes it is Mr. Ford," said Mrs. Kelly. "If you need anything, just write to me."

Sherman stood up.

"Okay."

Mrs. Kelly stood up and extended her hand out to Sherman. Sherman shook her soft hand.

Captain Lok stood up, "Let's go."

Captain Lok walked from behind the table. Sherman followed him back to the lockdown unit. The inmates were still making a lot of noise, yelling and banging on their doors. Sherman walked into his cell and gathered his belongings. He followed Captain Lok to a metal door. Captain Lok opened the door and the sunlight poured into the building. Captain Lok and Sherman stepped outside of the building. Captain Lok pointed to the third building from where they stood.

Sherman nodded his head. "Okay, I see it."

There were inmates walking around on the compound.

Lok said, "Stay out of trouble down there."

Sherman looked at the Captain, and then he started walking down the compound. Four inmates walked past Sherman. The men wore street clothes. No one spoke. As Sherman got closer to two inmates who were standing on the compound, he could see that those men also had on street clothes. One of the men was a short chubby white man with dirty looking brown hair. He wore a white tank top and had a lot of tattoos on his arms. The other man had medium brown skin and was thin in build. He stood at least six foot two. He wore a gray cotton sweat suit with black high top tennis shoes.

The white man was the first one to speak. "What's up, Bro?"

Sherman didn't respond. Then the other man spoke.

The black man said, "Slim, you looking? I got [1]dime bags of caine."

Sherman just kept on walking. When he got to the entrance of his unit, there were eight young black men in their late teens and early twenties laughing and playing. All of the men wore street clothes. Sherman pulled the metal blue door open and walked inside of the dorm.

The walls and floors were brown, just like the walls and floors of the other buildings, but these walls and floors had graffiti on them. Sherman walked to another door and pulled it open. He just stood in the doorway and was amazed at the atmosphere. A thick cloud of smoke filled the air. There were metal bunks everywhere. Inmates were walking around half dressed, some were fully dressed. Radios and TVs were blasting. There was laughter and yelling all around the room. Some of the men looked toward the door when it opened.

Sherman just walked over toward his bunk. A lot of men watched him. A few of the men spoke to him when he got to his bunk. He just laid his belongings on the bed and sat down at the top of the

---

[1] "Dime" means a ten dollar portion of drugs.

bed. He looked at the neatly made bunk in front of him. No one was on the bed. Then Sherman looked at the guy lying on the bunk behind him. The man was in his early forties with a little gray in his hair. He was dark skinned in complexion. The man was lying on his bunk with his hands folded across his chest and his feet were crossed. He had his eyes closed but Sherman could tell the man wasn't in a deep sleep.

A medium built man with freckles on his face walked in between Sherman's and the resting man's bunks. Sherman looked at the man.

The man spoke, "What's up, Playa? I'm just trying to get past," said Freckles.

Sherman didn't speak back. He just moved his feet to the side. The man walked on by. Sherman made up his bed then he went outside. The young dudes were still outside talking. Sherman stopped and looked at one of the young men. The man gave Sherman a mean stare. The other men stopped talking and looked at Sherman with calm eyes but with a stare that showed a readiness to kill.

The man Sherman was looking at spoke, "What's up, Joe?"

The young man looked half Spanish with his light complexion and short silky but curly hair. His name was KT. He was short with a small build.

"How do ya get to the yard?" asked Sherman.

KT's facial expression eased up.

"You new?" KT asked.

"Yea." Sherman replied.

"Look Joe, we're getting ready to go to the yard. You can walk with us. Where are you from?" KT questioned.

"Northeast." Sherman replied.

"What part of Northeast?" asked Shorty.

Shorty was also light brown skinned. He was medium build with a bald head. His nickname matched his height.

"Near Paradise." Sherman offered.

Shorty looked at Chop. Chop was medium build, dark skinned with a low haircut. Chop stood about the same height as Sherman.

"Chop, he lives around your way," said Shorty.

Chop said, "I've never seen him.*"*

Sherman didn't respond.

"Y'all ready to walk," asked Shorty?

"Let's roll," said Gangster.

Gangster was medium height, thin in build with straight Indian hair. Gangster was a pretty boy with dark skin. The five men started walking toward the yard. They walked in silence for a few minutes.

Then Gangster spoke, "Playa, what's your name?"

"Sherman."

"I think I heard your name being talked about on the street. How much time you have?" asked Chop.

"Five to fifteen."

"You don't have long before you go home. You should be getting ready to go up for parole soon. Is this your first bit[2]?" asked KT.

"Yea."

When they entered the yard, Sherman thought he spotted John. He wasn't sure. The guy looked to be in his early forties with a medium build and a light beard like John used to wear.

Sherman stopped walking and looked over at the dude he thought he knew from the street. Everybody else stopped beside him.

"What's up, Sherm?" asked KT.

"Nothing, I just spotted someone I know."

"Well, look; we are getting ready to circle the track. You walking with us?" asked KT.

"Nah, I'm going to holla at my buddy."

"Well, we'll see you around," said KT.

"R-right, Playa."

KT and his friends walked over to the track. Sherman looked over at the man that he believed he

---

[2] "bit" refers to amount of time someone has served in prison.

knew. Once Sherman realized it was John, he started walking over to him.

John was holding a conversation with six other inmates beside the bleachers. As Sherman got closer to the men, all of them except John looked at him. Sherman spotted Moe pulling something from his back and held it down by his leg. John turned around with an evil look. Once John recognized Sherman, he started smiling. He walked over to him laughing and they shook hands.

"Damn Sherman, what in the hell are you doing here!?" John humorously questioned.

Sherman was also smiling.

"Nigga, I'm doing a bit!" said Sherman.

John was so happy to see his friend, that he couldn't believe it was him.

"Damn! Sherman, when did you get down here?"

"Two weeks ago."

"Where you been then?"

Sherman looked serious now, "I got caught up in some shit. So, they locked me down."

John's face became serious, and then he turned around to face his other friends.

"I'll be back. I'm getting ready to talk to my peoples."

The men all nodded their heads in agreement. John turned around to Sherman and put

*his left hand on Sherman's shoulder and turned
towards the track. Sherman turned around.*

"Let's take a walk around the track," said John.

*John was in his late thirties with a muscular
build with salt and pepper hair and beard. He was
brown skinned with hazel eyes. Both men stepped on
the track and began walking along the track. There
were also a lot of other men on the field and in the
courtyard. John had his hands around his back. He
tilted his head sideways to look at Sherman.*

"So what happened?" John asked with concern.

"Some bitch ass Niggas robbed me for my tennis
shoes when I got off the bus."

"Yea, have you seen them today?" John asked
casually.

"Nah" Sherman replied.

"Look, what dorm are you in?" John questioned with
a hint of concern in his voice.

"Unit three, five dorm" Sherman replied.

"Damn, that's my dorm too. Sherman, I'll get you
some steel[3] tomorrow." John excitedly said.

"Cool."

"Sherman if you are a hard sleeper, tonight stay up,
and watch what be going on in the dorm. Then you'll

---

[3] "Steel" is another term for prison knife. A knife
is also called "Shank".

know to sleep light. Keep your boots on your feet at all times. Sherman, you can't trust these dudes. All the crooks and killers they take off the street, they are in here. So always watch your back."

"Cool," said Sherman

"How much time you have?" asked John.

"Five to fifteen"

"That's not much. When you spot one of the dudes who robbed you, let me know and I'll get on top of that."

"John, I can handle mine." Sherman replied.

"I know but I have been playing by these rules longer than you, so you have to trust me." John demanded.

KT walked up.

"What's up, Killa John?" asked KT.

KT was smiling at John. John shook KT and his friend's hands.

John was smiling when he spoke, "What's up, KT!?"

"Ain't shit. I see main man Sherm is walking with you," said KT

"Yea, he's my peoples."

"Well, you know how we go. So if you have a problem, let us know, Sherm," said KT.

"Cool."

"R-right ya'll. We'll holla at y'all in the dorm," KT said to Sherman.

"R-right KT," said John.

KT and the others walked away.

"Them are some good youngens. They are all cold hearted killers and they stay in shit. They probably stabbed over a hundred dudes in here. It's a whole mob of them, too. If, you beef with one, you are beefing with all of them. They'll get in a dude shit quick, too," John bragged to Sherman in a matter of fact tone.

"Yea, I walked with them down here. They broke their mugs[4] down at me at first."

"They're really some good young dudes. They don't bother nobody but a lot of butt bandits[5] used to pick with them until they started cutting their hearts out. Now everybody speaks to them and keep on walking."

"When I came over there to you, the big black dude pulled his knife out." Sherman questioned.

John started smiling, "My main man, Moe. Moe love pushing[6] that knife. Them youngens love him cause

---

[4] "breaking" or "broke" mug down" means frown or gritting on someone.

[5] "butt bandits" means men who rape men in prison.

[6] "pushing or pushing that knife" means to stab

he stay in some shit! He is a good dude, too. I'll
introduce ya when we get to the unit."

*Then something that sounded like a bullhorn
started blaring.*

 "Come on, its body count time," said John

*John and Sherman walked back to the unit.
They had to stand by their beds until the guard came
past and counted them. Sherman walked down to
bunk thirty, which is John's bunk. Moe slept in the
bunk across from John. John and Moe both were
sitting on their bunks facing each other talking.
Sherman stood at the foot of John's bed.*

John looked up at him, "Sit down Sherman."

Sherman sat on John's bed.

John spoke, "Moe, this is my peoples, Sherman. I
was just telling you about him."

"What's up?" asked Sherman.

Moe looked over at Sherman and smiled.
He had a missing tooth. His smile looked crazy.
Sherman didn't know if he should smile or what.

Then Moe spoke, "Have you ever ate blood,
Youngster?"

*Sherman was shocked at the question and he
didn't know how to respond.*

"What!?" Sherman replied with a puzzled
expression.

John and Moe started laughing. Moe stuck out his big muscular arm and hand. Sherman had never seen muscles in a man's hand. He had on a T-shirt that was so tight that his muscles were bulging out. His arms were as big as logs and he was as black as midnight. Sherman shook Moe's hand and Moe gave him a firm shake. Sherman gave Moe an insidious smile. Moe smiled back as he released his hand.

"Youngen, we're going to get you some steel tomorrow." Moe sternly said.

"My name is Sherman, Moe."

Moe held up his hand like he was blocking a punch, smiling.

"Okay, Sherman." Moe said.

"Give him a break, Moe..." said John. "Sherman, don't you pay this fool any attention."

Moe got serious.

"Yea Sherman, I'm just joking with you."

"I heard that you had a little girl by Ella," John said to Sherman.

"Yea" Sherman replied.

"So how are they and how is Moms doing?" John questioned.

"They alright." Sherman said.

They talked until 1:00 AM. Then John and Moe laid down and Sherman walked to his bunk and fell asleep. Sherman woke up because he heard someone trying to scream. It seemed the screams were being muffled. He looked to his right and saw one man holding a pillow over his bunk buddy's head, while another man was stabbing him viciously. Sherman wiped his hand over his eyes to make sure he wasn't dreaming. After he wiped his eyes, he saw the same thing that he saw at first but now the man being stabbed was not moving anymore. Then one of the men said something to Sherman.

"Go ahead back to sleep, Sherm."

It was KT. Sherman just sat up and shook his head. Gangster was with KT. Both men had walked off by the time Sherman sat up. Sherman snatched up his boots one at a time and shoved his feet into them. When he looked up, he saw a guard about eleven bunks away, shining lights in the faces of the inmates. So Sherman hurried up and lay back down so he could play sleep. When the guard shined the light on the man who had been stabbed, he saw all the blood. He pulled out his walkie-talkie and called for back-up. About twenty other guards came running into the room a few seconds later. The light had been turned on. Two guards grabbed Sherman, slammed him down on the floor and handcuffed him.

"Man, what the fuck are ya doing?!" asked Sherman

One of the guards shouted at him, "Shut up!"

They took Sherman with them. They questioned him for two weeks. Then they decided he didn't do it so they let him go.

Chapter Three

Sherman walked back into the dorm and down to bunk twenty-eight. John now slept beside the bunk on Moe's right. John was lying on his back reading a book. Moe was making up his bed. Moe looked up at Sherman and smiled.

"Hey! Sherman!"

Sherman smiled at Moe. John sat up when he saw Sherman.

"What's up, Big Moe?" asked Sherman.

Sherman threw his belongings on his bunk. The guy who slept in the bunk over Sherman was asleep. Sherman walked over to Moe and they shook hands. Then Sherman and John shook hands.

"What's up, Playa?" John asked.

Sherman responded, "Nothing much."

Moe lifted up his bunk bed and pulled out a balled up towel. He handed Sherman the towel.

"This is your Christmas present," he said.

Sherman unrolled the towel. There was a nine inch knife in the towel. The knife had tape around the handle. It was made from part of a metal window. Sherman put the knife in his waistband.

"Don't cut your prick off, that thing is sharp!" said Moe.

The man that sleeps over Moe just jumped up on the top bunk. Moe looked up at the man and rolled his eyes.

"I can handle this."

"Sherman, go get your bunk together so we can head to the chow hall[7]," said John.

"Got that."

Sherman went and made up his bed. The three men walked outside heading toward the kitchen. It was a nice noon summer day; birds were flying above their heads. There were about a hundred men on their way to the chow hall to eat lunch. Sherman heard an airplane flying above his head. He looked up just in time to see the plane fly into the thick white cloud. Moe held the door open when they got to the chow hall allowing the men to walk in and get in the chow line. Sherman was standing behind John, who was standing behind Moe in the line. The inmates who worked in the kitchen were putting food on their trays as Moe and the others slid their trays past the different foods. The Bread Man unintentionally tossed Moe's bread on his tray. The Bread Man had a brown skinned complexion, medium build with a long scar on his neck. Moe looked at the man with an evil stare.

"Nigga, what the fuck is wrong with you!?" yelled Moe.

The Bread Man snapped back, "What!?"

_____

[7] "chow hall" is another name for the kitchen or dining area.

"Bitch! You heard me!" Moe barked back.

"Man, fuck you!" The Bread Man said as he stared daringly into Moe's eyes.

"What!? Nigga, stay right there!" Moe sneered.

Moe started to walk around the counter to The Bread Man but John grabbed his arm.

"Moe, let that shit go. Fool don't know what he's getting himself into," said John.

Moe pointed at his tray.

*"M*an, you see how he threw my food on the tray!?" Moe said.

"Let him live," John said.

Moe then pointed at the man. "I'm going to get you."

The Bread man smirked.

"Whatever, you got your bread, so roll out!" he replied.

Then Sherman snapped at the man. "Shut the fuck up! You're about to let your mouth get the rest of your neck sliced off!"

The man looked up at the ceiling then back at Sherman.

"Man, do you want some bread or what?" He said nonchalantly.

*John slid his tray in front of the man. He put
two slices of bread on John's tray. John looked at
Moe who was still looking at the man.*

"Get your food, Moe," John said.

*Moe shook his head at his new enemy. Then
they went on down the line getting their food. The
three men went and sat at the same table where KT
and his friends were sitting.*

*The long brown tables could seat at least
forty people on each side. There were seven of these
tables filled with inmates. The walls were the same
colors as in the other buildings. KT was seated right
across from Sherman.*

When KT saw Sherman he spoke, "What's up,
Sherman? I apologize about you going to the hole
for my beef."

"Don't trip off that, Playa," said Sherman.

"Did you receive the food I was sending down?"
asked KT.

Sherman said, "Yea, good looking out."

"It was the least I could do. You are aight right
now?"

"Yea, I'm cool."

"I had to get that bitch ass nigga. He tried to talk to
my girl before I came into the visiting room."

"Yea," said John with a look of bewilderment.

"Then he wanted to talk shit to me. Man, I don't know what type of time these dudes are on, but I ain't the one to fuck with," said KT.

"I hear that," said John smiling.

KT looked at John and smiled. Moe was still frowning.

"What's up, Big Moe?" asked KT.

"Nothing, but I want to tear this bitch head off," Moe said.

"Who, Moe!?" asked Gangster.

"Bitch ass nigga who was passing out the bread."

"What's up, Moe? You trying to get at him now?" asked Chop.

"Chill out, Chop. Leave that shit alone," said John.

"I'll catch him, Youngen," said Moe.

Then the men began eating their food. Moe had peeped out the side of his left eye. He saw two dudes coming down the side where KT and Gangster were sitting, holding shanks at their side.

Moe whispered to KT across the table, "Its two dudes moving in your direction. They're holding."

All the men looked out the side of their eyes at the two men, who were now about thirteen feet away.

"Oh, that's the bitch ass dude I smacked this morning," said KT.

John said, "Let's work."

Sherman and nine other men stood up and pulled out their knives. The approaching men stopped in their tracks and looked at KT and his friend. Then one of the men spoke to his buddy.

"Let's roll."

Both men were surprised to see them stand up like that. The two men backed up about ten feet before they turned around and walked out of the chow hall.

"Let's go," said KT

"KT!" John called.

KT stopped and looked at John.

"Eat. Don't chase those fools. They're not going anywhere."

"They going to try and hit me up," KT said.

"We'll get them," said John.

"R-right," KT acknowledged.

Then they all sat down to eat.

KT looked at Moe. "Moe, you have some good ass eyes."

"Any man who can't see in the dark is a dead man. It is a must, I see everything," said Moe.

"Moe have eyes like an owl," said John

"And the heart of a bear," Moe said.

"Sheeed! That's bullshit! That woman has your nose wide opened and your eyes pouring tears," joked John.

They all started laughing.

"Big Moe, you have a girl?" asked Chop with a look of surprise.

"I was fucking when you were still in your pop's nuts!"

They all laughed.

"That's fucked up!" said Chop laughing.

"Are y'all ready to roll out?" asked John.

"Yea, let's get out of here," said Sherman.

They all got up and carried their trays to the trash cans. They threw away their trash and put their trays on the tray rack. When they were walking back to their housing units, they saw the two men from the kitchen with handcuffs on, walking with the guards.

"Them bitch niggas checked in," said KT.

"Don't trip," said John.

"Damn," said KT. "I wanted to get my man tonight."

"KT, how much time do you have?" asked Sherman.

KT spoke proudly, "Three hundred and two years."

Sherman exclaimed, "Damn! What did they give you the extra two years for?"

"Picking a lock" KT said with a broad smile.

"Man, that is a lot of motherfucking time!," said Sherman.

"Sheed. I'll be home in about thirty years." Chop said half jokingly.

Sherman couldn't believe his ears.

"Thirty years!!" said Sherman. "Got damn! You sound like that is around the corner. That is a long ass time."

"I'm trying to get back on my appeal now." KT said in a softer tone as if he regretted bragging.

"How old are you," asked Sherman?

"Eighteen." KT muttered.

"Damn, Playa I sure wish you luck on that appeal." Sherman replied.

They walked back into their dorm. They all stood and sat on or around Moe's, John's and Sherman's beds. Moe and Sherman's names were called for a visit. Moe opened his treasure chest at the head of his bed and pulled out his prison clothes. Moe started putting on his prison clothes.

"Why are you taking off your clothes and putting on prison clothes?" asked Sherman.

"You can't wear street clothes in the visiting room," said Moe.

Sherman asked, "John, do you have a mirror?"

John went into his treasure chest, pulled out a mirror, and handed it to Sherman. Sherman pulled out a comb and combed his hair. Moe stuck his mirror on the side of his bunkmate's bed. John was watching Moe look into the mirror. KT and the others were laughing.

"What the fuck are you doing, Sleeping Beauty!?" asked John.

They all broke out in laughter.

"Gots to look good for [8]my bun," said Moe.

Sherman came and stood between the bunks beside Shorty. Moe looked over at Sherman.

"You ready, Sherman?" asked Moe.

 "Whenever you are," answered Sherman.

Moe threw the mirror back into his treasure chest, and then looked at Sherman.

"Let's roll… I'll holla at the rest of you dudes when we get back."

Moe and Sherman headed to the visiting room. Moe was strutting with his arm swinging like he was a pimp. John and the others were laughing at him.

---

[8] *"Bun" is a term men use in prison meaning girlfriend or wife.*

"Work, Playa! These people don't have shit on you!" said Shorty.

They all continued to laugh. Sherman and Moe walked outside. They had to walk across the compound to get to the visiting room. Moe started singing while they walked. Sherman looked at him with amazement. Sherman didn't know the man could sing.

"You have to learn to respect! The power of love! I was a victim of my foolish thinking," sang Moe.

Moe continued the song until they got inside the visiting room building. Then both men were searched. They walked into the visiting room and sat down. The room was half full with a lively mixture of adults and children visiting their loved ones. There were about ten picnic tables with four chairs for the inmates and their visitors to sit in. There was a man holding a toddler and a seven year old in his arms while his woman stood smiling beside him. They were standing in front of a sheet that dangled from the wall. A picture of a forest had been painted on the sheet. It was being used as a background for when the inmates took pictures with their friends and families. The camera man is also an inmate.

Moe and Sherman sat at different tables. Moe's girlfriend came in first. She was in her late thirties, medium build. She had a beautiful figure. She had a light complexion. She wasn't as tall as Moe. She walked over to Moe and they kissed passionately. Sherman was amazed at how pretty she was. He considered Moe very unattractive. Sherman just shook his head in disbelief. Moe and his girl sat down and began talking.

Ella and Loretta walked into the visiting room. She was a medium height woman with a smooth deep dark complexion. She had an hour glass figure with large eyes that matched her smile. Loretta was her mini-me.

Sherman stood up and looked at them smiling.

Loretta pulled her hand away from Ella and ran over to Sherman. Sherman scooped her in the air and planted a big kiss on her cheek. She giggled. Then he sat her little body down in a chair. He smiled and pulled Ella's waiting lips to his. They kissed passionately. Then they locked hands as they took their seats. Her smile was amazing.

"What's up, Baby!?" asked Ella smiling.

Sherman was also smiling, "Missing you, that's all."

"I miss you too... I tried to come and see you last week, but they said you were on lockdown, so your visits were cancelled. What's going on, Baby?" Ella said with great concern, "This is the second time this has happened. I tried to see you when you first got down here but they said the same thing they told me last week."

"This guy that slept next to me was killed. So they questioned me for two weeks. They knew I didn't do it but they tried to get me to tell on who did."

"Do you know who did the killing?" Ella asked with a quizzical expression.

"You know how I feel about that."

"Sherman, I don't want you to get into any trouble. I want you home with me and Loretta." She replied.

"Daddy, when are you coming home?" asked Loretta.

"Soon, baby girl." He said with a wide smile.

"You going to come to my birthday party, Daddy?"

Loretta asked with a hopeful smile.

Sherman looked at Ella.

"Damn, I forgot her birthday is tomorrow. So, when are you going to give her a party?" he asked.

Ella said, "This Saturday. Your mother wants to have the party at her house."

"So are you going to do it there?" she questioned.

"Yea." she replied.

"Daddy, are you coming!?" asked Loretta.

Loretta had a big smile on her face. Sherman didn't want to break her heart but he didn't want to lie to her so he told her the truth.

"Loretta, Daddy won't be able to come to your party. I have to stay here a while."

Loretta looked like she was going to cry, "Why, Daddy!? I want you to come."

"I can't come Boo, but when I come home, me and you are going to have a big party, okay?" He replied with a reassuring smile.

Loretta didn't look relieved, she spoke in a low voice, "Okay, Daddy."

Sherman felt bad that he had made her sad. Ella saw the disappointment on both of their faces. Ella grabbed one of Loretta's hands and rubbed it with her thumb.

"Loretta...me, you, and Daddy are going to have a party when Daddy comes home." Ella informed. Then Ella looked at Sherman, "Boo, she's going to be alright." she said to Sherman.

Sherman expressed his disappointment in himself.

He spoke sadly, "Ella, it's her fifth birthday, and I can't even be there. Damn! I fucked up. Just look at her. She's really hurting because I can't be there, Ella."

Ella still spoke in a soft voice, "She's going to be alright...When do you come home... in five years?"

"Nah, should be sooner than that. I go up for parole in six more months." he revealed.

"Do you think they'll let you come home?" She replied in excitement.

"I doubt it, but I'm not sure. Hopefully, they'll cut me loose." he said with doubt.

"Do you need anything?" she asked.

"Yea, I need some clothes. Send me a pairs of boots, too." he replied.

"What can you have?"

"Three pants, three shirts, and three pairs of tennis shoes. I need a coat, too." he said.

"I'll buy you some new stuff tomorrow and I'll send all of it before the party. I'll drop you off a few dollars out front... Do you know anybody in here?"

"Yea, John is down here." he replied.

"John who?" she looked puzzled.

"John Neils."

"Oh, how's he doing? I haven't seen him in about four years." she said smiling.

"He's doing alright. Me, him, and that big guy taking that picture with that woman, be hanging together."

Ella looked over at Moe and the woman hugging him while the camera man took their picture. Then Ella looked back at Sherman.

"He's big and black."

Sherman started smiling.

"Yea, he's a good dude though and the bama can sing."

Ella changed the subject.

"I'll be back up here Sunday, okay?"

The guard sitting behind the desk yelled out Sherman's and Moe's names. Moe and the woman had sat back down at the table. Moe looked over at the officer.

"What's up!?" Moe shouted.

"Your visits are up!" said the guard.

"R-right," said Moe.

Moe and the woman stood up and kissed each other passionately again. Sherman looked Ella in her eyes.

"Well, it's time for me to go back to my unit."

Ella looked sad now. Sherman ran his right hand across her cheek.

"Come on now, Ella. You'll be up here Sunday. Please do not start crying."

Then they both stood up and kissed. Sherman kissed Loretta on her cheek and then kissed Ella again. Ella and Loretta turned and walked out of the visiting room. Sherman watched them leave sadly. Moe walked over beside him.

"I hate to see them go too but they'll be back," said Moe.

Sherman let out a deep breath, "Yea."

Then Sherman looked at Moe

"When you go home, Moe?"

"In about five more years." He replied.

"How long have you been down[9]?" Sherman questioned.

"Eight."

"Damn! She been with you the whole way?" said Sherman.

"Yup, the whole way." Moe said proudly.

"Damn! That's good. She did the whole eight years with you?"

"I know she's getting her needs taken care of, but I'm not tripping off of that. That's her pussy. If I was out, I would be fucking. So I expect her to do her own thing. She gets down here and she takes care of me."

Then the guard walked over to them, "Come on so I can strip y'all and get y'all back to the unit."

They followed the guard to the back of the visiting room where they had to strip. Then they were sent back to their units.

_____

[9] "been down" means how long have you been locked up.

Chapter Four

Sherman and Moe came up the walkway to their unit door. KT and eight other young men were in front of the door talking. They all shook hands with Moe and Sherman when they reached the door.

"What's up, Playas!? Did you both enjoy seeing your loved ones?" asked KT.

"Yea, I have to say, it was quite nice. I really enjoyed myself," Moe said smiling.

"Moe has a beautiful woman," said Sherman.

"What'd you expect? Two ugly people don't mix. I know I'm an ugly motherfucker but I keep a pretty female," said Moe.

"Moe, man you are crazy!" Chop said.

"Man, I have to get out of these cheap clothes. So I'll see you youngsters later," Moe said.

"R-right, Playa," said Shorty.

Moe opened the door and went inside. Sherman grabbed the door before it closed. Then Sherman looked at Gangster and the rest of his new friends.

"I'll see you fellas in a minute," said Sherman.

"R-right, Playa," said KT.

Sherman walked into the dorm and down to John's bed. John was sitting up with his color TV in between his legs. He was watching the soap operas.

"What's up, John?" asked Sherman.

John looked back at Sherman then he looked back at the television.

"I'm watching my soaps. Did you enjoy your visit?" John asked.

"Yea, Ella said Hi."

"How is she?" John questioned.

"She's okay. Loretta is mad at me because I can't make her birthday party."

"Yea. That's one of the rough parts of being locked up. She'll feel better once the party starts. Don't let it get you down." John suggested.

"Where did Moe go?" asked Sherman.

"Moe went into the shower."

"He has a beautiful woman." Sherman informed.

John spoke, never taking his eyes off of the television, "Yea, she's gorgeous. I don't know what she sees in that creature."

"She is alright fo' real though… I see you are on those soaps hard."

John pointed at the TV. "Yea, these are my women," he said proudly.

When they heard some arguing, they both went to the end of the bed to see what was going on. Four men were standing by one man's bed arguing with him. The man stood with his back against his bunk and his hand behind his back. John touched Sherman on his shoulders. Sherman looked at John, and then Sherman looked back over at the man.

"They are not going to push the knife in him," said John. "If they were, they would have done something by now. They're bluffing."

"Dude has one of his hands behind his back. He might have a knife." Sherman suggested.

"Nah, he's bluffing. He would have used it by now, too."

The man with his hand behind his back swiftly smacked one of the men up side his head with a lock in a sock that he had hidden behind his back. Blood squirted out of the man's head as he sprinted out of the dorm. John, Sherman, and a lot of the other inmates laughed at the man fleeing. Moe came running out of the shower with his towel around his waist and his knife in his hand. The buddies of the man that was hit with the lock in the sock started swinging on the man. They beat him down to the ground. Then they stomped him with their feet. When the guards came running into the dorm, Moe walked over behind someone's bunk. The guard locked the three men up and carried the other man out on a stretcher. KT and the others strutted into the dorm after the guards left. They all were standing around John's bed. Moe had put his clothes on. Then they all began talking.

"Why did they whip that dude?" asked Shorty.

"I thought they were bluffing. Then the dude bust one of them in the head with a lock in a sock. Man, when dude got hit with that lock, that ass ran out of here like a bullet," said John.

They all laughed.

"I thought y'all was beefing," said Moe.

"I saw you run out that shower like a wet gladiator!" laughed John.

"Fuck you," said Moe.

They all broke out in laughter.

"Y'all trying to go outside?" asked Sherman.

"Sure, let me get my boots on," said John.

"We'll meet ya'll out there," said KT

"R-right," said Sherman.

While John was putting on his tennis shoes, Gangster and the other young dudes went outside. John stood up and shook his left leg.

"Ya ready?" asked John.

"Let's roll," said Moe.

John and the others walked into the courtyard. KT and the others were leaning on the side of the bleachers talking to some other men. John and Moe shook hands with the men. Sherman saw Howard the brown skinned man who robbed him of his tennis shoes leaving the yard.

"That's one of those bitch ass niggas who robbed me."

"What? What's up, Sherm?" asked KT.

"Who did you say that was?" asked John.

Sherman pointed to a man in a red sweat suit. The man was the only one with a red sweat suit on walking in the crowd of people who were leaving the yard.

"That bitch ass nigga in the red sweat suit?"

"Let's get him!" said Shorty.

One of the other older dudes named Snake spoke.

"Youngster, calm down. The dude sleeps in housing unit one, dorm one, and bunk thirty-three. You can catch him in the dorm." Snake suggested.

"Let's roll," said Chop.

"Chop, y'all come through the east door," said John. "And we'll go through the west door. That way we will block him off."

"R-right. Let's roll," said KT

KT and the other eight teenagers walked out the courtyard heading to the dorm.

"Man, them youngens are crazy," said Snake. "I haven't seen nobody so eager to kill somebody. I'm just glad they're on our side."

John shook Snake's hand.

"See ya later."

"R-right," said Snake.

Sherman, John and Moe walked to the dorm. As they entered the dorm, they saw that KT and the others had all ready gotten to the man.

"Them damn youngens don't never want us to have no fun," said Moe.

"Let's go see the body," said John.

The three men walked through the crowd of people. They saw the man in the red sweat suit and another man lying in a puddle of blood dead and another man sitting on the floor holding his side. The man was screaming, "Somebody go get help!" He had been stabbed in his ribs. The two dead men looked like they had been tortured.

"I'm getting ready to take the other chump out," said Moe.

"I didn't have no beef with him," said Sherman.

"So what!" exclaimed Moe, "He must have gotten in the way? They probably thought they had finished him off."

They saw a knife stick through the crowd behind the man. The knife came slamming down into the man's scalp. Moe turned his head in disgust. Whoever had the knife in their hand shifted it to the side before pulling it out. The newly dead man's body shook and blood spouted out of his head. The knife disappeared back into the crowd. John spotted

Gangster walking out of the dorm. Sherman spotted him, too.

"Them youngens don't care. I thought I was terrible, but I ain't shit," said Moe.

John smiled at Moe and said, "Let's go."

The three men turned around and walked out of the dorm. They walked back to their own dorm. Then they saw KT and about fifteen others sitting around their bunks, laughing.

John said, "Let's go over there."

The three men walked over to KT's bunk. They shook all of the men's hands.

"You youngens have gone crazy!" Moe said.

KT started laughing.

"Why didn't y'all wait for us?" asked John. "Y'all knew that was Sherman's beef."

Gangster said, "Sherman's beef is our beef you know how we go."

"Next time wait or save me some," said Sherman.

KT said, "Cool, you will get the next one."

"Why did y'all hit the other two?" Sherman asked.

"They must have drew their knives. They didn't know," John said smiling, "but fuck'em."

"Somebody told you dude wasn't dead, Gangster?" asked Sherman.

"Nah, I always stick around to see what happens."

"That's how your ass got locked up!" said Shorty.

They all laughed.

"Good thing I did stick around because he almost made it," said Gangster.

"Nah," said Moe. "I was about to get to him."

"You move too slow," said Gangster. "But I know you would have got him."

"You damn right I was," Moe responded.

Moe sounded angry but he wasn't. None of them could tell if he was serious but John.

"Calm down, Playa," said KT.

Moe spotted The Bread Man. Moe pointed to him, "Hey Sherman, ain't that The Bread Man?"

Sherman looked over at the man, "Yea that's him, what is he doing, selling sandwiches?"

"I don't know but he's about to get his ass whipped!"

Moe pulled his shirt over his head and handed it to John then he looked at Gangster.

"I'm going to show you how to rumble, Youngen."

Moe started walking toward The Bread Man. The Bread Man was talking to another man lying on his bunk.

"Come on ya!" said KT. "Let's make sure this Joker doesn't try to run."

"Come on! Hold up! This is Big Moe's fight, so keep your knives in your pants. Let's roll," said John.

The men walked over to the far end. While Moe headed straight toward The Bread Man. He turned around and saw Moe coming toward him. The Bread Man then sat his paper bag down on the bunk and he pulled a real kitchen knife from his waist.

"You want to take the easy way, huh!?" asked Moe.

John yelled, "Slim, you better put that knife away!"

The Bread Man looked around him and saw all of Moe's friends with their knives visible.

"This is hand-to-hand combat we want to see!" said John.

All the other inmates were bunched up between the bunks, trying to see what was going on. The Bread Man lifted his knife in the air then he let the knife drop to the floor.

The Bread Man said, "I like this!"

The Bread Man was smiling. Moe started walking toward him with his hands up and fist balled.

"Let's rumble!" said Moe.

The Bread Man pulled off his white kitchen jacket, revealing a tank top and a gold chain with a cross medallion. He was as muscular as Moe. He tossed the shirt on top of his bag and threw his hands up.

"Fight time," yelled John.

"Ding, ding, ding!" said KT, laughing.

The Bread Man threw a straight jab at Moe. Moe weaved the jab. Then The Bread Man faked a jab to Moe's face. Moe weaved again but The Bread Man cracked Moe with a right hook to the rib. Moe had stumbled backward and started bouncing on his tippy toes.

"Nice one!" He smirked.

"Nigga, you haven't seen shit yet!" The Bread Man bragged.

Shorty started laughing.

"Fuck that, I'm hungry," said Gangster. "I'm going to get those sandwiches."

Gangster walked over to the bunk and picked up the bag. The man sitting on the bunk looked at Gangster. Gangster gritted on the man, and then he walked back over to his friends. They all got sandwiches out of the bag. John started eating his sandwich immediately. Then John pointed at Moe laughing.

"Moe, body shots!! Throw body shots!" yelled Sherman.

Moe said, "I got him!"

Moe threw two punches that pounded The Bread Man in his face at the same time as he was hitting Moe with four shots to his body. Then he hit

Moe with a hook across the chin. Moe stumbled backwards almost losing his balance.

"I'm getting ready to put this knife in that chump," said Chop.

"No, this is Moe's fight," John warned.

"Man, he's beating the shit out of Moe," said Chop.

"Just watch," said John.

The Bread Man faked a left jab and caught Moe with a right hook on his chin, knocking Moe to the floor. He cocked his foot back to kick the shit out of Moe.

"I advise you to keep your feet on the floor," said John… "Come on Moe! Get up! Get him!"

Moe jumped up onto his feet and threw his hands up. He threw a left jab and a right hook. The Bread Man went under the jab and threw a hook. He then caught Moe with two body shots. Moe jumped back still holding up his hands. The Bread Man threw a left jab. Moe went under the jab and grabbed him around his waist. He jammed his shoulder up against The Bread Man's stomach and rammed the man's back to the edge of a bunk bed bar. The Bread Man screamed out in pain. Moe then forced his shoulder up against the man two more times. The man dropped his hands. Moe stepped backwards and rapidly punched him in the face six times before kneeing him in his groin. As he begun to collapse, Moe kneed him in his face.

John and everybody else were screaming wildly with excitement.

Moe wrapped one hand around The Bread Man's shoulder and placed the other in between The Bread Man's legs. He lifted the man in mid-air and threw the man's body, slamming it into the concrete wall. His body slid down the wall. Moe started kicking him wildly. Then somebody yelled, "Guards!!" Moe swiftly ducked in between the bunks.

The guards spotted The Bread Man's bloody body against the wall. They ordered everybody to their bunks. KT and Sherman gave each other a hi-five then they went to their bunks. When John and Sherman walked over to their bunks, Moe was laying flat on his stomach. John burst out laughing and smacked him on his back before going to lay down on his bunk. John and Sherman were still laughing at Moe. Moe looked at John. Moe was tired and out of breath. His eyes were blood shot red.

"Fuck y'all!" said Moe.

John started laughing even harder, "Good work, Playa!"

"Yea, you beat his ass, Playa!" said Sherman.

Moe put one finger over his mouth, "Shhh, the guards might hear you."

Moe spoke all out of breath. John was laughing so hard, tears were coming out of his eyes. After the medical people took The Bread Man's bloody body out of the dorm, one of the guards spoke.

"Listen up!" The guard shouted.

"Fuck you!!" Somebody yelled as laughter filled the dorm.

"Now if something else happens in here tonight you will be put on lock down!" shouted the guard

Somebody yelled, "Fuck you, Bitch! You better get out of here before I put a knife in your bitch ass!!"

"Who said that!?" the guard demanded.

Then the same voice yelled, "Your Mother, Bitch!!"

"Now I have warned you!!" The guard proclaimed.

The guards left the dorm. Everybody in the dorm started moving around again. Gangster and the whole crew came around Moe's bunk.

"Nice work, Moe," said Chop.

"Yea, you got your man," said Shorty.

"After that youngen got tired of beating his ass!" laughed John.

Everybody burst out in laughter.

Moe still was out of breath, "Fuck you, John."

KT stood over Moe and he spoke in a serious voice.

"Moe, I'm going to kill that dude for you."

Moe looked up at KT

"No, K. I want to fight him again."

"That's right, Gangster!" said John. "Get back at him."

"Moe, if you change your mind let me know," said KT.

"If I change my mind, I will kill him myself," said Moe.

Sherman patted Moe on his side.

"Ouch! That shit hurt," said Moe.

They all started laughing.

"Good rumble, Moe," said Sherman.

Moe turned over and laid on his back smiling.

"Yea, I jive[10] got my man tonight."

"Nah," said John, "You got your ass beat! That's what you got tonight!"

Moe threw his towel at John.

"Fuck you!" said Moe.

"Won't you lighten up on the man," said Sherman.

"Sheed! If I was the one fighting, he would be making more fun of me than I am of him."

---

[10] "jive" means "some what"

Then one of the guards spoke over the intercom.

"Lights out, Gentlemen."

The lights in the dorm were turned off. As Chop and their crew said goodnight to John, Sherman, and Moe, they all walked over to their bunks. John, Sherman, and Moe were all lying across their bunks on their backs.

John looked over at Moe. "Are you all right though, Playa?"

"Yea, I'm cool. In a little pain though."

"Can you cut on the radio tonight?" asked John.

John could only see Moe's white teeth glowing in the dark.

"Oh, Yea."

Then Moe turned toward Sherman.

"Youngen, break out your tissue, cause we're going up town."

"Let's go, Baby," said Sherman.

"Distant lover! Lover... Lover... Lover..." sang Moe.

"Work Playa," said Sherman.

"...So many miles away. Heaven knows I long for you tonight. Distant lover... You know I think about you sometimes. In this place, every moment I spend with you is a treasure,   like a precious jewel. Say

65

you love me. Love me; Love me, Please, Please.
Please come back Baby," Moe sang with passion and
conviction as he remixed it with some of his own
words. He sung into the wee-hours of the night.

Chapter Five

"Sherman," said John. "Get up. Get up, Sherman."

John was shaking Sherman's body. Sherman rolled over on his back and looked up at John in wonder.

"What's up!?" Sherman replied half awake.

"Man, I told you about sleeping hard." John grumbled.

Sherman sat up in bed, and then he ran his hands across his eyes.

"What the fuck did you wake me up for?"

"Are you still going to the truck or what?"

"Oh, yea. Damn! What time is it?"

John looked at his wristwatch, "9:45AM."

"What time do we go to the truck?" asked Sherman.

"Whenever you get ready."

"R-right," said Sherman. "Hold on a minute."

Sherman looked in his treasure chest and grabbed his toothpaste, toothbrush and washcloth. He went into the bathroom and freshened up. He then walked over in between Moe and John's bunks. Moe was digging through his treasure chest. John was putting on a pair of tennis shoes.

"Y'all ready?"

Moe and John looked over at Sherman.

Moe's left eye was swollen and he had a bruise on his nose. "What's up, Sherm?"

"Nothing at all. You alright? You jive bruised up."

"Yea, I'm cool. I wonder what he looks like this morning."

They both laughed at the thought of how badly beaten The Bread Man must look.

"He probably can't even see himself yet," said Sherman.

Moe started smiling with pride written all over his face, "Yea."

"Sherman, do you want an outfit and some tennis shoes to put on?" asked John. "I know you're tired of those prison clothes."

"Yea I'm tired of these clothes but I'm alright. Ella supposed to go and buy me some new shit today."

Moe stared at the back of the man's head that slept above his bunk. He was sound asleep.

Moe screamed at the sleeping man, "Get up!!"

The man rolled over and had angrily looked Moe straight in his evil eyes.

"Moe, stop playing, man," said his bunk buddy.

"Nigga, get your bitch ass up! You always sleep! Get the fuck up!" Moe shouted.

"Moe, get out of my face." The irritated and half awake man replied.

"What!!?"

"Moe, I am not scared of you," said his bunk buddy.

Moe spread his arms out in the air, "What you want some rec!?"

"Moe, go ahead man. I'm trying to sleep. I don't fuck with you when you are asleep."

"Cause you are a punk."

When Moe said "punk," some sprinkles of spit from his mouth splattered on the man's face. The man took his hand and wiped his face. Then he shook his head.

"Damn man, you spit in my face."

"If I did something wrong, punch me in my mouth!" Moe shouted.

"Come on Moe," said John. "Let's roll."

"When I get back you better be up and ready to fight."

"Yea," said the bunk buddy. "Whatever."

The man turned his back to Moe. Moe raised his hand as if he was going to smack the man but John grabbed his wrist.

"Come on, Moe," said John.

"R-right! Man, what you turned into, some kind of peacekeeper?" Moe said, bitterly.

"Yea. I'm trying to keep that man from whipping your ass."

John started laughing then the three men walked out of the dorm. It was cloudy outside and the air was cool.

"Damn, it's chilly out this joint," said Moe.

John started rubbing his bare arms..

"No bull."

As they walked down the compound, a few other convicts spoke to them. Some of the men congratulated Moe on winning the fight last night. Moe smiled and nodded his head in acknowledgment. Once they were near the canteen truck, they saw three men robbing another man for his bags of food. One of the robbers held the man by his shirt and held a long, sharp shank under the man's neck. His partners took the man's two bags of food. The robber who held the shank ordered the man to walk back toward the canteen truck. He did as he was told. Then the robbers walked in the direction of Sherman and his friends. Sherman tensed while John and Moe continued to talk as if nothing happened. The robbers spoke to John and Moe as they passed them. Immediately, Sherman, John, and Moe heard someone running at top speed behind them. They spun around in fighting stance to see a man running for his life. Chasing him was Gangster and Chop.

70

"What the fuck are those youngens doing now?" asked John.

As the man nearly passed them, Moe snatched him by his neck. He pulled the man to his chest and held him in a chokehold. Moe started smiling and rocking the man. The man's tongue was hanging out of his mouth as he struggled to breathe. Gangster and Chop came to a stop in front of them.

Moe said, "Don't do nothing! I got him!"

Moe was steady rocking the man. The man's eyes started rolling in the back of his head.

John started shouting, "He's going! He's going to sleep! He's going! He's gone!"

The man became unconscious. Moe tilted his head to the side. He was trying to see if the man's eyes were closed.

"He's out, Moe," said Chop.

Moe released his victim's body. The man's lower body crashed to the concrete before his head slammed in to it. He made an irritating sound. Eight guards came running toward them.

"Get down! Lay down on the ground!" yelled the guards.

"Man, fuck you!" said John.

The guards surrounded the five men.

A medium build white guard spoke, "Neil, what happened?"

John said, "We saw him lying on the ground knocked out. We were on our way to the canteen truck."

"The tower guard said somebody was choking this man." Corporal Stevenson said.

Officer Daniels started shaking the man's body, "Wake up. Wake up."

"I don't know nothing about that," said John.

Daniels shook the man again. This time the man's dazed eyes opened.

He wiped his eyes. Then he looked up at everybody, "What happened?"

Two of the guards helped him to his feet.

Stevenson asked, "Before you went unconscious, do you remember who was giving you trouble? Was it any of these five men, or were they all picking with you?

The man wiped his eyes and shook his head then he pointed at Gangster.

"He tried to rob me." The man said, in an exhausted voice.

"Bitch ass nigga, I didn't try to rob you!" Gangster shouted.

Stevenson said, "Lock him up!"

Two guards grabbed Gangster. He didn't resist. One of the guards handcuffed him. He was mad as hell. You could see it in his face as they did.

"Were any of these other men involved in trying to rob you?" asked Stevenson.

"Nah" the man replied

"Are you sure?" Stevenson asked

"I'm positive."

Stevenson looked at Gangster, "Son, I know you weren't alone, who was with you?"

Gangster broke out in laughter. Then Stevenson looked at the injured man.

"Go back to your unit." Stevenson

"Man, I'm not going back to my unit!" the man shouted.

"What!?" Stevenson was irritated.

"Ya taking me with ya."

Sherman and John started smiling.

"What are you doing, checking in?" Stevenson humorously replied.

"That's right." the injured man confirmed.

Everybody started laughing except Stevenson; he was holding his laughter back.

"Okay, cuff him, too." Stevenson ordered the guards.

One of the guards cuffed the man.

"Dude, you're a cold bitch!" said Gangster. "What in the fuck you get locked up for!?"

"Nigga, what in the fuck are you talking about!? I'm locked up for murder."

Moe burst out laughing.

"Ooooh, he is dangerous!" said Chop.

The guard who had been talking to the man started laughing.

"You men go on where you were going." Stevenson ordered.

"Playa, I'll send you down," said Chop.

Gangster said, "R-right, keep the pressure on these suckers while I'm gone."

"That's a must!" said Chop.

"Put me down as your representative at your hearing," said Moe.

John said, "Put all of us down as witnesses."

"R-right," said Gangster.

"Go where you were going now," the guard said.

Chop gritted at the man and turned around and started walking. The rest of his friends were following close behind him.

"That chump told!" John said. "I can't believe that shit."

"And he says he's a killer," said Moe. "I don't know where they get these chumps. I don't know who would let a chump like him kill them."

"That bullet ain't no sucker. Bullets were made to do the destruction. It just takes anyone to pull the trigger and any chump can do that," said Sherman.

"Yea," said John. "That's true."

Chop shook his head in disbelief.

"Man, I can't believe that chump told on him," said Chop. "A lot of dudes are starting to snitch, on the street and off the street. A motherfucker can't get away with shit."

"It's called helping themselves now," said John.

Moe started laughing.

"Man, look at that shit," Sherman said.

Two men were walking toward them holding hands. They were an interracial couple. One man was a muscular bald headed, dark-skinned man. The other was an overweight white man with shoulder length blonde hair, eyeliner, dark lipstick, and his shirt tied at the bottom left. As the two walked past them, Sherman and the others watched them while shaking their heads in disbelief. The white man was switching his behind as he walked. Then he peered over his left shoulder and winked his eye at them. Chop had lifted his shirt to show the overweight man his knife. With instant fear in his eyes, the man directed his attention to where he and his partner were walking

"I'm going to kill that bitch when I see him again," said Chop.

"John!" Moe said smiling, "Who do you think is the woman?"

John snapped at Moe, "How in the fuck do I suppose to know!? They are probably fucking each other."

Sherman and Chop shook their heads at the thought of the two men having sex with each other.

"Man, this place is weird as shit," said Sherman.

Chop said, "I have to get the fuck out of here."

They all went to the truck and bought what they wanted to eat for that week. As they were walking back up the compound, they stopped to talk to KT and seven other young dudes.

"What! Ya on ya way to the truck?" asked John.

KT was smiling.

"Yea."

"I know that look. What's up?" asked Chop.

"We're getting ready to rob the joint," said KT.

"Man, ya have gone crazy!" said Sherman.

"Ya want something?" asked KT.

"K! Man, won't ya cut that shit out?" said John.

"Man, I'm hungry."

"Man, them motherfucking young girls be sending money orders up in here, so stop faking. You're going to fuck around and catch another charge."

KT was smiling when he spoke, "What are they going to do give me two more years?"

John just shook his head, "Me and you are going to have to have a talk."

"Where is Gangster?" asked KT.

"They locked him up," said Moe.

"What!?" Shorty responded.

"Yea," said Chop. "This bama said something slick out of his mouth. So Gangster smacked the chump then he broke out running. Moe grabbed the chump and rocked him to sleep. When the guards came, the dude pointed Gangster out. So they locked him up."

KT shook his head and looked at the ground.

"Damn man."

"I'm going to be his lawyer," said Moe. "He might go up for the ticket tomorrow."

A light rain started bouncing down on their bodies. They all looked up at the sky.

"Damn! Look," said Moe. "I'm going in."

Moe started walking swiftly back to his unit. John looked at KT

"Look, my food is getting wet," said John. "What are ya going to do, KT?"

"I'm getting ready to go take care of this business. The rain will make it sweeter. You going, Chop?"

"Yea, I'm with this." Chop replied.

"Well, I see ya later," said John.
KT asked, "You don't want anything?"

"You sound like you going to buy something," said John. "K, you're crazy, Playa. I'm all right though."

"When we hit," said KT, "we'll throw a party in the dorm."

"If you hit," said John, "we'll all be locked down tonight."

"Sheeed. At least we won't be hungry," said KT.

"Holla at me when you get back," said John. "R-right?"

"I'll do that," said KT.

KT looked at Sherman, "Sherm, you trying to go with us?"

"Nah, Playa. I'm going to sit this one out."

"R-right then. We'll see ya when we get back."

"Don't catch no bodies down there," said John.

"R-right," said KT. "Let's roll, Fellas."

The young men walked down the compound. The rain continued to fall. John looked at Sherman and shook his head.

"That time is kicking him in the ass hard," said John, "I'll talk to him, though. Let's roll."

The two men turned around and headed back to their housing unit.

Chapter Six

Sherman and Moe sat on Moe's bunk and John sat on his own bunk. The three men talked. The other inmates in the dorm were talking loud, laughing, playing or sleeping. The dorm lights were on as usual. Televisions and radios blasted. John started laughing at a story Moe had told them.

John said laughing, "Man, you're a sick dude! Why did you burn the woman with the iron?"

"That fool thought I was going to eat her pussy!" said Moe. "She was in heat and I burnt that ass up with that iron!"

Moe stood up and started jumping around holding his private part, laughing, "Ahhh! Ahhh! You burnt me! You burnt me, you crazy son-of-a-bitch! Man, the hoe was going crazy! Then the bitch just fainted."

"So what did you do?" Sherman asked smiling.

"Sheed fool!" said Moe, "I left that hot bitch on the floor! Sheed, what you think, crazy!? The pussy was smoking!"

They all burst out into laughter. John was laughing so hard, he started choking. Sherman patted him on his back. When John looked up he saw KT and about thirteen other men. They threw a whole lot of food onto John's bed. John looked at all of the food, and then he looked at KT.

John smiled, "K, you are a wild young dude."

"That ain't all of it. That's just for tonight, so eat up!"
"I got the music!" said Moe.

Moe blasted the radio up loud and started dancing. They all started laughing. Some of them sat on both beds. They were all bobbing their heads to the music. KT and John started opening up the food. Sherman stood up. KT looked at him in wonder.

"What's up, Playa?"

Sherman placed his hand to his ear and mouth like it was a telephone.

" I'll be back!" Sherman said.

KT nodded his head in agreement, "R-right. We'll be here when you get back."

Sherman turned around and walked from around the bunks. While Sherman was headed to the six phones on the wall at the back of the unit, Auto stopped him. There were other men seated and standing near him. They were engaged in conversation before Auto stopped Sherman.

"Hey Sherm," said Auto smiling. "What's up?"

Sherman smiled back and shook his hand.

"What's up?" asked Sherman.

"Ain't shit," said Auto. "Where John and Moe?"

"They're at the party," said Sherman.

"At the party?" asked Auto out of amusement.

"Yea. They're throwing a party at the bunks."
Sherman informed him

"Do they have any food?" Auto asked, seriously.

"Yea, lots of it." Sherman said, cheerfully.

"Sheed, I'm getting ready to go to the party then,
huh, Fellas?" Auto cheerfully said.

They all shook their heads yes.

"Sherm, you all right?" asked Auto. "Where you
going?"

"I'm getting ready to call my folks." Sherman
replied.

Auto patted Sherman on the shoulder.

"R-right then Sherm... You coming back to the party,
though?" Auto asked.

"Yea, I'll be back."

"See you when you get there." Auto said.

*Sherman nodded his head at the men and
went on his way. When Sherman got over to the
phones, they were all being used. So Sherman waited
until a white man got off the phone. He walked over
to the phone and picked up the receiver. He dialed
Ella's house. Ella answered the phone and accepted
the call.*

"Hold on for a minute, Boo." She said.

"R-right." Sherman replied.

Ella put the phone down for a few seconds. Sherman could hear loud music playing in her background and then the music went dead. Ella picked back up the phone.

"Hello." she said.

"I am still here." he replied.

"What's up, Baby?" She cheerfully said.

"Missing you," he said

"Aaaaaaw. I miss you, too" she gushed.

"What, you were having a party in there?" he suspiciously asked

"No... Loretta hold on. I'm going to let you speak to him.... Yea. Hello." Ella replied with frustration.

"What's wrong?" Sherman asked.

"Nothing. Loretta wants to speak to you." Ella said with a smile.

"Put her on the phone then," he replied.

"I'm going to let her talk to you... I sent your clothes off today. You should receive them next week." She said.

"R-right. What exactly did you get?"

"I got what you wanted.... Girl, get off me.... Hold on, Boo.... Here Girl."

Ella handed Loretta the phone.

"Hi Daddy." Loretta blurted.

"Hey Boo. How are you doing?" Sherman replied.

"I'm fine. My birthday party's tomorrow." she said excitedly.

"Happy Birthday, Baby. I love you." Sherman sung.

"I love you too, Daddy. Daddy?" she gushed.

"Huh!" he replied.

"Mommy bought you some clothes." she informed.

"I know, she told me." Sherman replied.

"I helped Mommy pick you out a dress." Loretta said proudly.

Sherman started laughing; he could hear Ella laughing in the background.

"Thank you, baby." Sherman replied.

"Daddy! You don't wear no dress! Dresses are for girls, Daddy!" Loretta said, seriously.

"I know." he replied.

Ella took the phone from Loretta. She got on the phone laughing.

"Boo, she is bad as hell." Ella said laughing.

"I see she's on joke time. I thought she didn't know the difference between a dress and a pair of pants." Sherman replied.

Ella was still laughing.

"Mmmm, she's terrible." Ella said jokingly.

"You are really getting a kick out of that aren't you?" he questioned.

Ella stopped laughing.

"I'm sorry." she replied with a serious tone.

"What are you sorry for?" he asked.

"I thought you were getting mad." she said, hesitantly.

"Nah... So is everything set for the party?" he said, trying to sound cheerful.

"Yeah... I'm going to take a lot of pictures and send them to you." she said excitedly.

"That'll work." he replied.

"I want you to take some pictures and send them home." she said.

"Whenever I get the clothes, me and John will take a picture or two." he said.

"A picture or two!?" she said with sarcasm.

"R-right, we'll take some pictures." Sherman laughed.

"Tell John to put my name on his visiting list so I can call him out and visit him too." she replied.

"R-right. He could use it. Nobody comes to see him. His family treats him so bad. They don't even write him," Sherman said in disappointment.

Micky a big muscular extremely light skinned man in his mid twenties walked over to Sherman. He just stared at Sherman. Sherman looked at the man, then he spoke into the phone.

"Hold on, Ella." Sherman stared at Mickey "Wha-What's wrong, Slim?" Sherman demanded.

Mickey had one of his hands behind his back and was gritting on Sherman.

"That's my phone," said Mickey.

"Yeah, R-right. You'll get it when I get off."

Sherman turned around and grabbed the phone. He put the phone to his ear and started talking to Ella.

"Yeah, I'm sorry," said Sherman. "What were you saying?"

"Why did you get off the phone?" asked Ella.

"Some dude wants to use the phone after me. So what were you saying?" Sherman said in his normal tone.

"Tell John to put me on his list so we can come and see him." she replied.

"R-right." Sherman replied.

Then Mickey spoke again, "Bitch, get the fuck off my phone before they be carrying your bitch ass in the Dewitt truck!"

"Whoever that is, is he talking to you?" asked Ella.

"I think so."

Sherman turned his head to look at the man. The man was holding a shank in his hand.

"Bitch, get the fuck off the phone! Tell that hoe, bye!" Mickey barked.

"I'm going to call you back, Boo." Sherman firmly said.

"No! No… Don't…" Ella pleaded.

Sherman hung up the phone and turned around to face Mickey. The other men on the phone leaned away from the two men and stared at the two of them as they whispered into their receivers. Then two of the men hung up their phones and stepped out of the way. A lot of inmates were watching them.

"Now get the fuck away from my phone," said Mickey.

Sherman spoke in a serious yet calm voice. He had his knife in his waist but he knew the man wouldn't allow him to pull it out.

"Move me." Sherman sneered.

"Nigga, you better move before I put this knife in your bitch ass," Mickey threatened.

Sherman took his hand and motioned the man to him, but the man didn't move.

"Come on."

Mickey started loosening his neck by twisting it from side to side.

"What? You think I'm playing with your bitch ass?" Mickey said.

"You are not getting this phone unless you kill me." Sherman warned.

Mickey hunched his shoulder and started smiling.

"I guess I have to do what I have to do," he said.

As soon as the man took one step forward, Moe grabbed him around his neck and stuck a knife in his back. The man screamed in pain as Moe twisted the knife inside of him. John stepped in front of Mickey and started stabbing him in his chest. As John stabbed, Moe twisted his knife in the man's body. Mickey's eyes closed and his body started to convulse. Moe released the dead man's body. It fell limp to the floor. KT and the others came running through the crowd with their shanks in their hands. They looked down and saw the dead body.

"Damn, we're late!" said Chop.

"Yup," said John.

Moe bent down beside the man and wiped his knife off on the man's' shirt, then John looked at Sherman.

"You finish with the phone?" asked John.

"Yea," said Sherman.

They walked through the crowd that had formed. They all went back over to John's bunk. Moe cut the radio back on and started dancing. Nobody moved the body since the guards only enter the dorm during count time.

All of the inmates were so used to seeing dead bodies, that they left soon after John and everybody else left. When the guard came through at the eleven o'clock count, he ordered everybody to stay on their bunks. The medical people and a guard with a camera came into the dorm. There were also twenty other guards who came into the dorm. While the camera man took pictures of the dead body, the captain turned around to the inmates and started talking. The captain was a tall black man with a beard and a bald spot at the top of his head.

He said, "I do not know what the hell happened here but all of you will be on lockdown until I find out who killed this man. So, I advise you, if you know who did this, speak up. Nothing will happen to you. All I want is the person who is responsible, for this man's death. So what is it going to be?"

The guard looked around and the inmates didn't say a word.

"It's fine with me!" said the Captain. "You all are on lockdown until I find out who did this! You are nothing but a bunch of scared suckers!"

Somebody yelled out loud, "Fuck you!!"

"You bad? Show yourself!" said the Captain.

The captain looked around at the inmates again, nobody moved.

"I thought you were a chump, whoever you are!!"

The voice yelled again, "Fuck you, You bitch ass nigga!!"

All of the inmates started laughing. This made the captain even angrier.

"Shut up!! All of you!!"

The men laughed even harder. Then a lot of them started yelling out all kinds of statements. The Captain became consumed with fear, but he didn't let it show. So the Captain turned around to the nurses holding stretcher..

"Clean this mess up!"

As the Captain headed toward the exit, he kept looking side to side in every pair of eyes he could find as he passed the inmates until he was out of the dorm.

After the medics carried the body out of the dorm, one of the guards spoke.

"You all heard the Captain! You are all on lockdown and if I catch you off of your bunk, you will answer to me!!"

Most of the men jumped off their bunks. The guards hurried up and got out of the dorm. The guards knew the inmates would have killed them next with no problem. Once the guards left, the men got back on their bunks. Sherman, John, and Moe laid on their backs on the bunks.

Sherman looked at Moe, "Moe, cut the radio on."

"R-right, Playa," Moe said before he started singing, "Babies going to cry when in need. A man doesn't cry even when his heart starts to ble-e-d! So when a man cries! He's giving you his soul. So when the tears start to fall and he's reaching out his hands. There's nothing more than the warm tears of a m-a-n! So let it be known when a man cries, he's giving you his soul. He's giving you his emotions. There's nothing more than the tears of a m-a-n."

They all fell off to sleep. At four o'clock in the morning, forty guards rushed in the dorm and arrested Moe, John, and Sherman. They found a knife near each of them. The guards informed them that another inmate sent a note stating that the three of them would be killed if they weren't removed from the dorm. The three of them stayed in the hole for two months. When they came off, the warden sent Moe behind THE WALL.

THE WALL is a super maximum prison located two miles away and the Warden sent John and Sherman to the prison known as The Hill.

The Hill was a maximum-security prison with six separate buildings. It was a mile away from the prison they were originally housed. There are eight different prisons on that land. The Hill is the deadliest one of them all.

When Sherman and John came out of the hole, they had beards and heads full of hair. The Hill had green cell bars. The bars stretched down the tier

for half mile. There were six levels of tiers in all.
There are three thousand inmates housed on The Hill.

Along with all of the other inmates,
Sherman and John had single cells. This prison
previously housed two men to a cell, but cell-mates
kept killing each other. So, they changed the policies
to one man to a cell. The cells were the size of a
small studio apartment. Some of the men had cats or
dogs, floor model TVs, stereo sets, curtains, and
pictures on the walls inside of their cells. The
institution allowed this to pacify the men and keep
the violence down.

Sherman and John both walked into their cells and
went straight to sleep after making sure their cell
doors were locked.

Chapter Seven

Sherman lay on his back with his hands behind his head looking up at the ceiling. Suddenly, a man's voice seemed to have spoken through the walls.

"Mr. Ford!" the voice of Corporal James' was heard over the intercom.

Sherman looked first at the bars, but no one was standing at the bars.

"Mr. Ford!" Corporal James voice rang out again.

Sherman then let his eyes drift around the room.

"What!? Who is that!?" Sherman questioned.

"Mr. Ford, you have a property room pass!" Corporal James shouted.

Sherman spotted the little intercom box on the wall beside the mirror. Sherman got up out of his bed and walked over to the toilet and leaned over to the intercom.

"What did you say!?"

"You have a property pass. Pick up your pass at The Bubble. It's the guard booth at the beginning of the tier." Corporal James commanded over the intercom.

"R-right. Give me a few minutes." Sherman replied.

Sherman's cell door slid open. He only had on boxer shorts and a t-shirt. He grabbed his clothes off of the metal desk and started putting them on. He then put his boots on and washed his face.

As he stepped into the tier, the place sounded lively, but Sherman could feel the deadly vibes of the grim, dingy and dimly looking place. He noticed that other inmates were walking up and down the tier. Sherman looked to his left, then to his right. He saw The Bubble at the end of the tier. He glanced up but had a hard time counting how many tiers were above his floor because of where he stood. He continued to glance around as he then started walking toward the booth. In his peripherals, he noticed other inmates watching him. Then John called his name.

"Hey Sherman!"

Sherman looked to his right and saw John leaning on the bars to John's cell. Gangster and another man were standing next to John looking at Sherman. The tall gentleman was medium build with a brown skinned complexion. The man looked to be in his late forties to early fifties. The man looked like a 70s wanna-be pimp. He wore blue sweat pants and a silk blue tank top. He also had two small gold chains around his neck. John and Gangster wore regular street clothes.

Sherman walked over to the men and shook Gangster's and John's hands. Then Sherman nodded his head at the other man. Gangster was smiling as he spoke.

"What's up, Playa?" Gangster said.

"Same old shit. So this is what they did with you," Sherman replied.

"Yup…" Gangster said nodding his head.

John interrupted them.

"Sherman, this is my man, Brace."

Sherman and the man shook hands.

"What's up?" asked Sherman.

"Getting money, that's all," said Brace.

"I can dig that," said Sherman.

"Were you about to go somewhere?" asked John.

Sherman replied, "Yea. I have a property pass."

Brace pointed to The Bubble.

"You pick your pass up from there," Brace said.

"R-right, I'll holla at y'all when I get back," said Sherman.

"R-right," said Gangster.

"Get yours, Playa," John said.

Sherman started smiling. Brace called his name.

"Sherman!"

Sherman stopped and looked at him.

"What's up?" Sherman replied.

"We might be gone when you get back, so come out to the yard!" Brace said.

"R-right."

Sherman turned back around and started walking toward the booth. He walked past six homosexuals who wore makeup. They were smiling at him. Some of them had on very short shirts that were rolled up to their navel. Three of them were black, two were white and the other was Hispanic. Diamond was the only one not wearing regular clothes. He was wrapped in a robe. He stood partially in his cell.

Sherman just shook his head and kept on walking. He glanced in one cell as he passed it. There was a man sitting on his toilet reading the newspaper. A lot of the bars had curtains covering the cells, so no one could see inside them. Music could be heard blasting from most of the cells.

Sherman walked over to The Bubble. Four guards were in it. When Corporal James saw Sherman standing in front of the window, he walked over to the window and pressed the intercom button on the control desk.

"Yea?" asked Corporal James, "What do you want?"

"You said you had a property pass for me!" said Sherman.

"Who are you," asked Corporal James?

"Sherman Ford!"

Corporal James turned to face Corporal Kritz and asked for the pass. Corporal Kritz handed him the pass. Corporal James held it up so that

Sherman could see it, then Corporal James pressed the intercom button again.

"Come around to the side door and get the pass out of the slot."

Sherman walked over to the right side of the booth to the door, bent over and opened the slot. He pulled the pass out of the slot and stood up. Corporal James nodded his head at Sherman.

Sherman held his hands out in the air, "I do not know where the property room is."

Corporal James couldn't hear him so he pointed to the intercom. Sherman walked over to the intercom. Corporal James pushed the intercom button as he spoke through it.

"What is the problem?" Corporal James questioned.

"Man, I just got here. I don't know where the property room is."

"Go over to that gate. When I open the gate, just walk straight down the hallway. There will be a guard sitting behind a desk. The property room is the door right beside the officer's desk," said Corporal James.

"R-right."

Sherman turned around and saw the big green bar gate. The gate was about ten feet away from the booth. When the gate opened, Sherman walked through. He came to a second gate that was closed He looked to his right and saw two gray doors that had a sign written on it that read, 'Exit'. When the first gate closed, the second gate opened.

He walked through the gate. Sherman continued down the hall passing doors that were either opened or closed.. He was stopped midway by Corporal Hicks behind the desk.

"Where are you going?" Corporal Hicks barked without moving.

"I have a property pass."

Corporal Hicks extended his hand, "Give me the pass."

Sherman handed him the pass. Corporal Hicks glanced at the pass, and then he wrote something down in a large blue ledger. He then looked back up at Sherman.

"Go on in." He said dismissively.

Sherman turned the door knob and went inside of the property room. The property room was a big room with a counter that divided the room. One side of the room was where the inmate's property was received. The other side was the designated waiting area for the inmates. Two inmates were retrieving their belongings that were sent from home.

Susan, a very attractive white female officer was distributing the property. When Sherman came into the room, the woman glanced at him, then back at one of the inmates in front of her. She looked back at Sherman and smiled. Sherman glared back and went and leaned against the back wall. When the other two inmates left the property room, the officer called Sherman over to the desk. She was still smiling at him as he approached. Sherman took note of her voluptuous breasts and pretty hazel eyes. She was a medium build brunette.

Two inmates were working in the storage area behind her, stacking boxes. Susan stared at Sherman for a few seconds then spoke.

"How are you doing today, sir?"

Sherman spoke in a friendly voice, "I'm doing okay."

"How can I be of help to you?" asked Susan.

Sherman stared at Susan and she started blushing.

"I have a property pass," Sherman replied.

"Where is your ID?"

Sherman pulled his ID card from his pocket and handed it to her. Susan looked at it. Then she smiled at him.

"Well, Mr. Ford, I do have a package up here for you," she said.

Susan turned around and walked over to a table with a lot of boxes, televisions, and radios on it. As she had her back to Sherman, he couldn't help but to notice that she had a firm ass. She looked over her shoulder and caught him staring, she smiled. Then she turned around and put her hands on her hips.

"Mr. Ford, it will be a minute before you will get your package. I have to tell one of the inmates to look for it in the back room."

Susan checked in with the men who were stacking boxes behind her.

"Sly! Look for a box with Sherman Ford's name on it. When you find the box, bring it to me, please." Susan asked in her most charming voice.

"Okay!" Sly answered.

Susan walked back over to the counter, as she handed Sherman back his ID, she let her fingers rub across his hand. He looked Susan in her eyes. She continued to smile.

"Why are you smiling?"

Susan spoke in a low lustful voice, "I'm a happy person."

"Yea, I'm a happy person too, but I don't be smiling like you do." Sherman said in-between his wide smile.

"We're just two happy people, huh?" Susan said blushing.

Sherman just smiled at her.

"You have a pretty smile." she said.

"You have a nice ass," he said, smiling.

Susan started giggling, "You are something else."

"I only returned a compliment." he said.

"Yea, but you were straightforward." she said smiling as she shook her head in disbelief.

"What's wrong with that?" he questioned.

The woman shook her head.

"Nothing."

"You don't believe you have a nice ass?" he questioned.

"I know I can get wet fast," she glanced up at him.

Sherman's smile had widened even more.

"Hmmmm. Wooo-wee. You are the one who is something else."

Susan just smiled. Sly sat the box on the counter. He gave Sherman an evil stare, then he went back to working..

Sherman's smile vanished. "What's wrong with him?" Sherman questioned.

"I don't know."

Susan started pulling Sherman's clothes out of the box.

"Sherman, what cell do you sleep in?" she asked.

"Eighteen. Why?" he replied.

"I just asked."

"What? Are you going to come and see me?" he replied.

She looked up at Sherman smiling then she started separating his clothes.
"I might." she said as she swayed.

"What do you mean, you might?" he said, firmly.

She looked back up at him.

"I might come through there at count time. I have to do the three o'clock count. So, I might stop pass your cell and say something."

"If you can't come just to see me, don't stop to say hi." he said, playfully.

She just stared at him. Then she handed him his clothes. Sherman picked up his clothes without looking at her and walked out of the property room. He went in his cell, put away his clothes, and then collected a few items he needed for a shower.

Sherman had two lockers in his cell to put his clothes in and a desk to write on. John, Gangster and Brace came to his cell.

"What's up, Sherman?" asked John.

Sherman turned around to see his friends standing behind him.

"What's up?" asked Sherman.

"Did they give you all of your shit?" asked John.

"Yea."

"Here, I have something for you," said Brace.

Brace stuck his hand through the open cell door. He had a balled up towel in his hand. Sherman grabbed the towel from him and opened it. There was a ten inch knife in the towel. Sherman looked at the knife then he looked at Brace.

"How much do I owe you?" Sherman asked.

"You owe me nothing. We're family. Do you know how to use that?" Brace said with a smirk.

"When the chance comes, you'll see my work." Sherman said, smiling.

"Yea, well these bamas around here will give you plenty of work."

"This joint seems calm," said Sherman.

"So that means it's more dangerous now. Nothing that is calm is harmless. The most dangerous men in this prison are the quiet ones. Sherman, the first lesson about this Hill is, don't trust no one here. Not even if you are sleeping with them. A lot of men had their balls cut off that way," said Brace.

"Well," said Sherman, "I don't go like that. So that won't be a problem."

"Some people do... Well, look, I have to take care of some business. John, fill him in on what's going on. Oh, I sleep on the second tier, cell two forty-four," Brace said as he walked away.

"R-right," said John

Brace patted John on his shoulder and walked off.

"Look, this is the deal, said John; Brace is getting money in here. I'm trying to get paid too. He said he can make $2,500 a week! That's a lot of money." "Damn sure is," said Sherman. "So what's up?"

"He keeps running out of coke. You still have your connects?" John asked.

"Yea, so what's up?" Sherman replied.

"We can get busy." John replied.

"R-right." Sherman replied. "I'm not going to get nothing big in here. First, I want to see how fast the shit moves in. So, I'll get Ella to bring me a quarter."

"Do you think she will do it?"
"We will see, but how am I going to get that shit in?" Sherman said, confidently.

"Tell her to put it in some balloons and tie them up tight and small. You can go to the bathroom and stick them in you rectum," John suggested.

"Sheed! You done gone crazy!!" Sherman replied.

Sherman looked furious. Gangster and John started laughing. John held his arms and his palms up flat in a calming gesture.

"R-right! R-right!" said John. "You can swallow them and shit them out when you get back."

"Man, I'm not swallowing that shit! That shit might burst and kill me!"

"Nah, not if you tell her to do it right. That's better than the rectum," John said smiling.

"You motherfucking right!!" Sherman yelped.

John and Gangster burst out in laughter. John said still smiling, "So what are you going to do?"

"I'll let you know. Look, I'm getting ready to take a shower. Where are they anyway?" asked Sherman.

John pointed to the right.

"All the way down the tier. You'll see the recreation room. They're in the back of the recreation room. Look... We're getting ready to go outside, so when you get out the shower come out there."

"R-right."

John and Gangster walked off. Sherman walked into the dayroom. A television was positioned on a shelf on the wall. About twenty inmates sat in chairs in front of the television. Ten round tables, a ping-pong table and a pool table were strategically placed in the huge recreation room. All of the round tables were filled with men playing cards or dominoes. There were two men playing ping-pong.

Sherman walked to a door and pushed it open. There were six urinals lined up against the wall and eight toilet stalls across from the urinals. He walked to the back of the room and saw the showers. There was a big square space with twelve dangling shower-heads spread around the room. There was only one man in the showers. He was a muscular white man covered in tattoos. He watched Sherman as he walked into the shower area.

Then he turned his back to Sherman and shampooed his hair. Sherman took all his clothes off except his boxers and his boots. The other man wore slippers. Sherman began washing his body as he stood under the running water from the shower. He put his hands on the wall as he held his head under the shower. Sherman began to feel strange, so he turned around.

While wiping his eyes free of water, Sherman saw six Mexicans walk into the shower with shanks grasped in their hands. He immediately became afraid, but stood ready to fight, despite knowing death was certain. He secretly cursed himself for leaving the knife Brace gave to him in his cell. He stood there with his eyes locked on theirs as he awaited their next move.

The white man had his head under the water, still unaware of the potential danger. His focus was on washing his hair, eyes closed. One of the short Mexicans raised a finger to his lip, signaling for Sherman to be quiet. Sherman didn't respond but continued to maintain eye contact.

The Mexican crept over to the white man and stabbed him in his rib. The white man spun around, blindly shoving the man that stabbed him. The Mexican stumbled back than regained his balance. The white man quickly wiped the shampoo from his eyes as the Mexican cautiously moved back toward him. When he saw the man and the rest of his friends, he didn't know what to do. He attempted to run past the Mexican who stabbed him, but fell on the slippery floor. As soon as his body hit the floor, the Mexicans swarmed him like a pack of bees. They began viciously stabbing the man. He screamed, swung his fist, tossed and turned trying to escape. The attackers continued to stab him. His body stopped moving and the water carried the blood down the shower drain. When Sherman walked out of the showers, the Mexicans were still stabbing the man's limp body.

Later the guards discovered the body and immediately put the prison on lockdown for the rest of the day.

Chapter Eight

*When the cell doors opened for chow,
Sherman walked out onto the tier. He looked to his
left and saw Brace talking to Diamond at his cell.
Half of Diamond's body was visible outside the cell.
Far as Sherman could tell, Diamond had on women's
underwear and a T-shirt. He saw him rub his hand in
between Brace's legs. Sherman just shook his head.*

*Then John walked out onto the tier from his
cell. His living quarters were positioned a few cells
down but in the middle of Sherman's and Diamond's
cell. He spotted Diamond caressing Brace's groin. He
looked in the opposite direction and his eyes caught
Sherman's eyes and he smiled as he shook his head.
They walked over to each other and shook hands.*

"What's up?" asked John.

"Same ole shit," said Sherman.

"Why did they lock us down yesterday?" John asked.

"Some Mexicans killed a white dude in the shower."
Sherman replied.

"How do you know?" John asked curiously.

"I was in the shower. I thought they were coming for
me. I'm glad they weren't though, cause I was empty
handed." Sherman confided sarcastically.

John looked at Sherman seriously.

"Why didn't you have your knife with you?" John demanded.

"I don't know. I guess I slept on this joint." Sherman replied, boyishly.

"In here, you carry that knife like you carried that gun on the streets. You rather be caught with the knife than without it. Sherman, stop taking chances." John warned.

"Oh, them Mexicans showed me how dangerous this joint is. You don't have to worry about me leaving home without it again." he said, sarcastically.

Gangster walked down to them.

Gangster shook both their hands, "How is life treating you two?"

"We are living, so it must be all right, at least for the day," answered John.

"We're going to live forever," said Gangster.

"That shit sounds good!" said Sherman.

"Don't it?" asked John smiling.

Brace came walking over to them smiling from ear to ear.

"Ya ready to go to chow?" he asked.

"Let's roll," said John.

The four men headed down the tier. Diamond was still standing in the doorway of his cell door. He waved at Brace. Brace just smiled and kept walking. Sherman and the others saw this but didn't utter a word, figuring it wasn't any of their business.

When they opened the door to exit the building, all shielded their eyes from the blinding sunlight. It was extremely bright especially coming from inside a dimly lit building. There were at least three hundred prisoners walking across the compound headed to the chow hall.

Brace began talking, "Ya know a war just kicked off."

"Yeah," said John.

"Them Mexicans killed one of those Aryan Brothers," said Brace. "So retaliation is a must. Bodies will start dropping all around here, real soon. So ya stay strapped, and keep your eyes open."

"What does their war have to do with us?" asked John.

"As you already know, those Aryan Brothers most definitely do not like blacks. Now that they're mad, they may try to kill whoever they can, so none of us goes anywhere without each other. No showers, dayroom, telephones or nothing unless we are together," said Brace.

"Why haven't y'all killed those crackers already," said Sherman.

"It's not that simple. First of all, this prison is owned and being run by the white man. The Aryan Brothers might be white trash to some of these crackers but they all have two things in common; they are white and they hate whoever isn't white. Plus, they're about four hundred deep in here and they are all killers. You ever noticed a teardrop under their eyes? Well, those stand for, 'I killed me a nigger,'" explained Brace.

"I've seen a dude with one side of his whole face filled with teardrops," said John.

"He must be getting his man!" said Sherman.

"If I catch him, he's dead!" Gangster barked.

Brace said, "Calm down, Gangster. We have to live here together. You just can't kill one of those fools. I have a lot of dudes who will roll with us, but it has to be for a cause. Plus, them crackers are our best customers. But if any of them get out of line, we will punish them. Now those Mexicans aren't no suckers either. They're going to kill a lot of the Aryan Brothers and a lot of them will die. But that's their beef not ours. We just have to watch our backs."

"So what's up with the Mexicans?" asked Gangster.

"They don't like us either, but they're cool. You have to watch their sneaky asses. They will run down on a motherfucker like flies on a dead body. Now if you ever get into a beef with them, watch them. Those motherfuckers keep razor blades in their mouths and they know how to use them," explained Brace.

The four men went into the kitchen. They got their food and sat down to eat. The kitchen was designed like the kitchen at their former prison. Four of the Aryan brothers walked over to Brace, Gangster, John and Sherman. Sherman and his friends turned around as best they could from their seated position to face them. Devil, the leader of the Aryan Brotherhood white supremacy group spoke.

111

"Bro, we come in peace. I would like to discuss a certain matter with you. Can I sit down?"

Gangster sat the closest to Brace. Brace looked at Gangster.

"Gangster, can you move down some?" asked Brace.

"Sure," said Gangster.

Instead of Gangster sliding down, he stood up with both his hands in his pants holding his knife. Devil thanked Gangster with a nod of his head and then he sat down. Brace turned around to sit properly at the table and looked over at Devil. Devil had five teardrops trickling down the corner of his left eye and a tattoo where his left eyebrow used to be that read, "DEVIL" In the same location over his right eye was a tattoo that read, "666". He was of muscular build with blond short spiked hair, and he was covered in tattoos. He had both of his arms on the table as a gesture of peace and his face turned toward Brace's.

"Bro, you know why we went on lockdown yesterday don't you?" asked Devil in his Deep South accent.

"No," answered Brace, "but I'm trying to find out why. Why, you know?"

"Those Spics killed and raped one of my Brothers." Devil sneered.

"Yea? I didn't know that, but what does that have to do with me?" Brace said with very little interest.

"Bro, I just wanted y'all to know, we do not have any beef with the Brothers. But we're getting ready to eliminate all of those Mexicans. I just wanted to know where the Brothers stand in this? Devil asked, politely.

"Devil, we don't have any interest in y'all war, just as long as none of us get touched." Brace replied.

"Bro, like I said, we do not have any beef with the Brothers." Devil reassured him.

"Then you don't have to worry about the Brothers." Brace informed him.

"Well R-right, Bro."

Devil tapped Brace on the arm and then he stood up.

"Devil?" Brace said, curiously.

Devil bent back down beside Brace.

"What's up, Bro?"

Brace looked him seriously in his eyes.

"You have a lot of black teardrops." Brace said with his eyes locked with his.

"Bro, that's from a long time ago." Devil said in a remorseful tone.

"Okay."

Brace turned back around and started eating his food. Devil stood up. He and his comrades walked off. Gangster sat back down beside Brace.

"What's up, B?" asked Gangster.

John and Sherman were leaning over the table so they could hear Brace.

"He just came to say that they don't have any beef with the niggas." Brace said, sarcastically.

Gangster looked surprised and angered by Brace's remark.

"That bitch said that!?" Gangster barked.

Brace said, "Calm down, Gangster. He wouldn't speak to me like that. I just know those were his thoughts."

"So why did he pull you up about it?" asked Sherman.

"Because everybody respects me and he knows if Blacks got killed, I would get my man. I don't care what he said though, we must still stick together. I'mma pull up the rest of the brothers and let them know what is about to go down," said Brace.

"How did you know about the shower killing?" asked Sherman.

"I fuck with the [11]gumps. They know everything. Just like I know you were in the shower without your shank. Sherman, keep that on you at all times. You never know when you may need it." Brace warned.

"I jive slept on this spot, but those Mexicans made me a believer." Sherman replied.

_____

[11] "gump" means homosexual

"They even fucked the corpse!" Brace said, "those little dudes don't be joking."

"I didn't see them fuck him," said Sherman.

"Well, it is believed that they did. One way or another, I could care less." Brace replied.

"Let's get out of here," said John.

They all stood up and left the kitchen and walked back to John's cell.

"Man, I have to use the phone," said Gangster.

"Let's go ya'll," said Brace.

They made their way to the recreation room. Gangster got on one of the eight phones on the wall. John, Sherman, and Brace got three chairs and sat up against the wall.

"Sherman, did John put you down with what we're trying to do?" asked Brace.

"Yea," answered Sherman. "I'm down. As a matter of fact, let me go make arrangements now."

"R-right." Brace sounded pleased.

Sherman got up and went to get on the phone. Ella answered the phone on the second ring and she accepted his call.

"Hi Boo," said Ella. "I have been waiting for you to call. Did you receive your clothes?"

"Yea, I got them yesterday when I came off of lockdown." Sherman replied.

"Why didn't you call me yesterday then?" Ella said in disappointment.

"Because something happened and they locked us down for the rest of the day." Sherman replied.

"Oh... so how are you doing? Do you need anything else?" she questioned.

"I am feeling fine... I do need you to take care of something though." he said in a secretive tone.

"What is it?" her voice mimicked his.

"I need you to bring something down here for me," he whispered after glancing around at the other men using telephones.

"What is it?" she replied.

"I want you to beep Ed and tell him to bring a quarter of an ounce. Then I want you to bring it down here to me."

"What!!?" Ella shouted.

"Why in the fuck are you screaming in my ear!?" he snapped angrily at her.

"I'm sorry, but why are you asking me to bring drugs down there?" she responded.

"Because I want it. Are you going to do it or what?" he said with irritation.

"No." she snapped.

"Well, I have to go then." he replied.

"No! No! Don't hang up, Sherman!" she pleaded.

"Ella, you acting like you can't do that for me?" he said angrily.

"Boo, why you always doing that? Every time I say, no, you get mad. Boo, I want you to come home, I don't want you selling drugs anymore," she whined.

"So what are you saying? You're not going to do it? Look, you don't have to do it. I'm getting ready to call somebody else, Bye." Sherman replied.

"I'ma do it. I'ma do it!" she pleaded.

"R-right." he replied, smiling.

"Sherman… why you always doing that to me?" she whined.

"I'm sorry but I'm trying to take care of business. Listen up, beep Ed and tell him to bring you a quarter of an ounce. When you get the coke, if it's big, chop it in half. Then put it in a balloon. Tie the balloon up with dental floss, then when you get down here put it in your mouth and when we kiss, I'll transfer it into my mouth, okay?" he instructed her.

"Okay." she said, intently.

"Leave Loretta with somebody. Don't bring her with you." he suggested.

"Okay." she sounded relieved.

"I want you to beep Ed when we get off of the phone." Sherman said.

"Okay." Ella said, reassuringly.

"Then I want you to come down here after you get off of work, okay?"

"Okay, I will come after work." she replied.

"Look, I have to get off the phone, so beep Ed now, bye. Love you." he said, cheerfully.

"I love you too." she said, smiling.

   Sherman hung up the phone and went and sat down in his chair.

"What happened?" asked John.

"She's going to bring something down."

   Sherman looked over at Gangster. Gangster looked sad.

"Damn," said John, "I have to make a call, too."

   So John went and got on the phone.

"I'm getting ready to holla at my man at the card table," said Brace.

"R-right," said Sherman.

   Brace got up and walked over to the card table. He began to talk to a big fat white man. Sherman looked back at Gangster.

"What's wrong, Gangster?" asked Sherman.

"I just received some bad news." Gangster said in sorrow.

"Talk to me, Playa." Sherman replied.

Gangster looked at Sherman and he looked like he wanted to cry.

"My baby's mother was in a car accident yesterday. She is supposed to have my baby next month, man. Now she is only living because of a life support machine." he replied in almost a whisper.

"She's going to pull through. Don't worry, her and the baby will be fine." Sherman said in a forced upbeat tone.

"Her and that baby are all I'm living for. They are all I have out there." Gangster said sadly. He was staring down at the floor.

"Man, it's going to be alright. How long have you been locked up?" Sherman questioned.

"Seven months." he replied.

"I thought you had been in longer than that. How much time do you have?" Sherman said, cheerfully. "Two to six years." Gangster replied, still looking at the floor.

"You're getting ready to go home. She's going to be alright. She knows you're on your way out there. She's going to pull through." Sherman replied, still trying to sound upbeat.

"If she dies, I won't have nothing else to live for." Gangster replied.

"How old are you?" Sherman questioned.

"Seventeen." Gangster replied.

"Man, you have your whole life in front of you. You have a lot to live for. We both do. Me and you are getting ready to go home. Playa, we are going take our kids to the park together, just me and you and our little families." Sherman said, reassuringly.

Gangster started smiling.

"Yea, I like that."

"She's going to be alright though. You watch… her and the baby are going to be fine, watch. Women are very strong mentally. Why you think they never get locked up? Man, it's because they can think. We don't think." Sherman said.

"I know what you mean 'cause I was shooting and killing a lot of motherfuckers and she said, 'Roy, your dumb ass is going to go to jail." Now, look where I am." Gangster said, smiling.

"I told you women are very intelligent. See death is a thinking game. Watch her think her way out of death." Sherman boasted.

"Man, I'm going to pray for her tonight. I don't usually do no praying but I want God to be with her." Gangster said with the sadness returning to his voice.

"There is nothing wrong with praying. I even pray." Sherman confessed.

Gangster looked at Sherman with surprise written all over his face.

"Fo' real!?"

"Yup. There isn't nothing wrong with it." Sherman said, smiling as he nodded his head.

"I don't know how to pray. What do I say?" Gangster inquired.

"Say whatever is in your heart. Say what you feel. God knows and hears all your prayers." Sherman replied.

"So I can say anything?" Gangster sounded impressed.

"Yup." Sherman said as he nodded his head.

"Well, I'm going to pray for God to watch over her and my son." Gangster boasted.

"How do you know it's a boy?" Sherman questioned.

"The doctor told her. Yeah! There is going to be another Gangster in this world! Fo' real though, Sherm, I don't want my son to live like me. I want my son to have a life." Gangster said as he looked Sherman seriously in his eyes.

"Well, you have to be a father, not a gangster. Your son is going to want to do what you do. You can't tell him what you do is wrong, but he sees you doing it. You will have to change, Gangster." Sherman warned.

"I can do that. I'm trying to get in school, well, they put me on the waiting list." Gangster said, proudly.

"That's good, Playa." Sherman replied as he smiled and nodded.

"I'm saying though, if a motherfucker disrespects me or my family, I'm going to kill that motherfucker dead." Gangster quickly warned him.

John and Brace walked over to the two of them.

"Let's go outside," John said.

The four men left the recreation room and headed to the yard.

Chapter Nine

The recreation yard on "The Hill" was actually the same as the recreation yard at Occoquan. John, Brace, Gangster, and Sherman walked over and sat down on the bottom row of the bleacher nearest the entry door to the building facing the football field. To the far left of the bleachers, men were in the weight area lifting weights, hitting the heavy bag and other kinds of exercises. Off to the far right was the black top where men were playing basketball on the courts.

John and the others started watching the two inmate football teams play. Both teams wore white football uniform pants and helmets, one team wore red shirts and the other blue shirts. The extra players and coaches were standing on the side of the field watching intensely.

Sherman took note that the prison guards were sprinkled out around the yard. The inmates outnumbered them thirty to one. There were two guards armed with shotguns scanning the yard from each of the four guard's towers positioned on each corner of the square recreation yard. Three guards stood close to the entry and exit doors to the building while a dozen other guards walked around the yard.

"I'll be right back," said Brace.

Brace got up and walked down to where a group of homosexuals were sitting on the bleachers. He sat beside Diamond. Diamond started rubbing Brace's leg while Brace was talking to him. Sherman and the others looked at him in disgust.

"John, what the fuck is wrong with that fool?" asked Sherman.

"Some like football. I like women and Brace likes men. To each his own." John replied.

"Doesn't he know crack kills!?" Gangster joked.

John started laughing.

"How long has he been in?" asked Sherman.

"Sixteen years." John informed.

"Good God O'Mighty!" Gangster said. "He has been in here almost my lifetime!"

"Yup," John responded.

"How much time does he have?" asked Gangster.

John replied, "Thirty to life."

"Damn!" exclaimed Sherman. "That is a long motherfucken time. Does he have to bring the thirty to the door?"

"Nah, he has to [12]bring nineteen years to the door before he goes up for parole," explained John.

"That is still a long time," said Gangster.

---

[12] "bring it to the door" means to do all of your prison sentence without getting paroled.

"Man, you have men in here who have been here forty years," said John. "Those men don't even think about the outside world anymore. Their families have died since they have been locked up. They don't have nobody to go home to. Whenever these people release them, they'll be back in prison in no time because society will scare the shit out of them. The streets have changed so much since they have been locked up. Society is constantly changing. When a lot of these men came to jail, Blacks couldn't even go into a lot of places. Now, we can just about go anywhere. Shit, forty years ago, there wasn't even any subways or a lot of shit that's out there now. These men won't fit back into society. They are so used to living and following the rules of prison. Now when they get back out in society, they're going to hurt somebody. I have even heard there was one dude who did thirty eight years! Now when they released him, he was back at the prison that same night banging on the door, hollering, 'Let me in.'"

"What happened?" asked Gangster.

"They didn't let him in! He was a free man. Since they wouldn't let him in, he went out and killed three people, then they let his ass back in for life. They should of never released that man without preparing him for society."

"I know he was crazy out there," said Sherman.

"I am not trying to go out like that," said Gangster.

John spoke jokingly, "You can handle it. All you have to do is get yourself one of the girls from around here and you're set!"

"Sheeed! said Gangster smiling, "As long as I have lefty and righty it's going to be all right!"

Gangster was holding up his palms so the two men could see them. John was laughing at Gangster. Sherman tapped John on his shoulder and pointed to the crowd of Mexicans, who were standing in front of Brace. John stood up.

"Let's go."

The three men walked down the bleachers and stood on the last row behind Brace. They held their hands in their pants gripped around their shanks. Sherman and Gangster were gritting on the Mexicans. The Mexicans returned the evil stares. A lot of other black inmates started walking over behind the Mexicans. Some of the Mexicans turned around to face the new arrivals, ready for war if it came down to it. Then one of the Mexicans spoke. His name was Carlos.

"Migo, there is no beef with you. There is no need for all of this. Carlos, just want to talk." he said to Brace as if he had recently started speaking English.

"They worry about me, Migo," said Brace. "You walk up on me with all your henchmen, my friends think you are about to hurt me."

"No, No, Migo," said Carlos. "We cool. You know that."

Brace nodded his head in agreement.

"I know, Migo, but you know things change."

"You do not like Carlos anymore?" asked Carlos.

"Carlos, you are still my amigo, but what's up? Talk to me."

"You know I cut one of those mothafucking white trash's throats in the shower?"

"Yea, Devil told me about that. You know he's mad with the Mexicans now?"

"Migo, fuck him! I'm gonna eat his tongue after I kill him."

Carlos was serious.

"So why have you come to me?"

"I heard Devil came to you in the chow hall."

"That's true."

"My beef is only with the Aryan Brotherhood, not the Blacks," Carlos responded/

"We do not have a beef with the Mexicans either."

"I thought they came to you for help," asked Carlos.

"You know I don't fuck with them. They hate us."

"They hate Mexicans, too." Carlos smiled.

"Migo, I wish you luck with the war," Brace added.

"Migo, I'll kill all those white trashes," Carlos replied.

"I wish you luck."

Brace sat down. Carlos and his henchmen walked off. The other blacks went back to doing what they were doing. Sherman, John, and Gangster sat down beside Brace.

"Why are they pulling you up like you are dangerous?" John said smiling.

Brace smiled back at him, "You haven't heard?"

"Heard what?" asked John.

"I *am* dangerous."

Giggling, Sherman said, "This joint is wild."

Then Chris, a small-framed black man walked over to Brace. Brace looked curiously at him.

"What's up, Chris?"

"Brace, do you have a dime?" asked Chris.

"Yea," answered Brace.

Brace dug in his pocket and pulled out ten small clear bags with crack cocaine in them. He handed Chris one of the small bags. The man held the bag up to the sun and looked at it.

Brace became mad and stood up, "Bitch, give me my money and get the fuck away from me!"

Chris nervously dug in his pocket and pulled the money out. He handed Brace the money and hurried up and walked off. Brace sat back down.

"These motherfuckers are going to make me kill somebody!"

Brace looked at Sherman, "Man, did you see that stupid motherfucker!? He held that shit up in the air like it was going to get bigger! I should have smacked the shit out of him."

John patted Brace on the shoulder.

"That's not good for business," John said.

Brace looked at John in disbelief.

"Yea whatever! Nigga, don't you know I know you!? You would have killed that dumb motherfucker! Who the fuck you think you're fooling?"

"Nigga," said John, "you better fix your tone of voice when you're talking to me!"

John looked serious and Brace noticed it. Brace played it off by laughing. Brace then looked at Sherman.

"You see what I'm saying?" asked Brace. "He's a cold killer! He knows I know this!"

"You two have gone crazy," said Sherman.

"Sherm, didn't you say your girl is going to bring some shit down soon?" asked Brace.
"Yea, she will be down here tomorrow," said Sherman.

"That is good because these nine-dime pieces of coke is all I have left." Brace explained with urgency.

"What's up with your connect?" Sherman asked.

"That motherfucker acts like he is not trying to bring shit to me anymore. Plus, he only brings me an ounce every three weeks. That shit is sold in a week. I want to start getting at least an ounce a week."

"Check this out, said Sherman, I told my girl to only bring me a quarter of an ounce tomorrow. I want to see how fast we can move that. Then I will get something bigger in here. I'm not going to keep jeopardizing my girl, so we are going to have to find someone to bring it down here. Plus, we are going to have to find a better way to get that shit in 'cause I'm not going to keep taking the risk. Getting the cocaine isn't a problem. The problem is getting that shit in here."

"Tell whoever is going to bring it down to give you their name," said Brace. "Then I will get one of my bitches to put their name on their list. One of the Queens can stick it in his ass and bring it in. What's up with the white bitch?"

Sherman looked at him in wonder, "Who?"

"The guard I saw at your cell talking a hole in your head," said Brace.

"I don't know those people like that." Sherman replied.

"Get to know that ho. She likes you now. Fuck her and get her to bring the shit in for us."

"That isn't a bad idea," said John.

"Man, y'all trying to send me to jail," Sherman said with anger in his voice.

"If you fuck the bitch, make her pay," said Brace. "Sell that dick, everything is business. Tell that ho', no finance, no romance."

All of them were laughing, except Brace.

"Brace, that woman is not tripping off of me like that," said Sherman. "She just wanted some conversation."

"When a bitch wants to talk, you feed her boxers full of dick and balls! The ho' is a cop. We don't have no love for them ho's," said Brace. "Dick 'em and leave 'em alone."

"We can use her though," said John. "Sherman, he has a point. Just try to get the pussy."

Sherman was grinning, "Yea R-right."

"Don't kiss and don't eat her," Brace said.

"What!?" exclaimed Sherman. "She can't get this head!"

"I don't know about you young dudes, ya be freaks," said Brace. "Ya be having bitches pissing on ya and tying y'all up."

"Sheeed!" said Sherman.

Brace looked at Gangster, "Gangster is a young freak. Tell him, Gangster."

Gangster was grinning as he started rapping, "Fool, I'm a gangster. I pimp whores and slam Lexus car doors. I fuck them, duck 'em, and if they get in my way, I pluck them!"

Gangster made his hand resemble a gun and pulled the trigger. They all busted into laughter. John was laughing so hard that he held his stomach.

"You ain't no gangster!" Brace said smiling.

Gangster raised his arms out in the air.

"They say gangsters are either dead or in jail. Shall I say more?"

Sherman was smiling up at Gangster then Brace called Diamond as he was walking past them.

"Hey Diamond!"

Diamond turned toward Brace and the others and put his hands on his hips. When Diamond spoke he sounded like a woman.

"Haaay, What's up?"

Brace parted his legs and started smiling.

"Come here, Bitch!"

Diamond looked up toward the sky and laughed. Then he started switching his behind and walked over and stood in between Brace's legs. He wrapped his arms around Brace's neck and threw his right leg over Brace's. Then he looked down at him.

"What's up, Daddy?"

"I want you to do me a favor." Brace replied flirtatiously.

Diamond started smiling.

"My cell or yours?" Diamond moaned.

Sherman shook his head and walked away. Diamond looked at Sherman walking away and rolled his eyes then he looked at Brace.

"What's up with him?" Diamond said in disappointment.

Brace smiled up at Diamond.

"He doesn't understand I got love for you, Baby."

Diamond started giggling like a female then he kissed Brace on his cheek.

"What do you need me to do?" Diamond replied.

"I want you to kill somebody for me." Brace whispered.

Diamond looked serious now.

"Who?"

Brace started smiling.

"I'm just kidding."

Diamond was shaking his head side to side as he spoke.

"Daddy, you know I don't have no problem with killing a motherfucker, especially for you." Diamond boasted.

"I know... All I want you to do is bring some coke back from the visiting room. Can you do that for me?" Brace said as he caressed Diamond's back.

"Of course I would. You know I love putting objects in my ass, especially, when it's that big dick of yours." Diamond replied as he started bouncing his butt on Brace's leg.

John and Gangster were looking at the two of them in disbelief.

Brace was laughing "You are something else."

"You haven't seen shit yet. Wait until I come down to your cell tomorrow morning." Diamond gusted.

"I'll be there." Brace said as he patted Diamond on his leg.

Diamond pulled his leg from over Brace's leg and stood straight up.

"Just give me the name, okay," said Diamond.

Diamond kissed Brace on his cheek again.

"Okay." Brace replied.

Then Diamond walked off. Sherman came back over to them and sat down. Brace looked at Gangster.

"You see what I said about the weak," said Brace. "You see how ready he was to kill for me?"

Gangster shook his head in agreement. A medium built dark skinned man walked over in front of Brace.

Brace looked up at the man, "What's up, Paul?"

"I need nine, ten pieces," said Paul.

"I have that."

"Brace," said Paul, "Check this out; I'm waiting for a two hundred dollar money order. It should be here tomorrow. The whole thing is yours if you let me get the nine joints now."

Brace looked up at him seriously.

"I'm going to give that to you. Now if you don't have my money, you will hang yourself."

Paul was smiling and shaking his head in agreement.

"R-right, but I will have that for you tomorrow." Paul said, reassuringly.

Brace said seriously, "R-right. You heard what I said."

Brace pulled the cocaine out of his pocket and handed it to the man. The man walked away. Then about thirty Aryan Brotherhood members walked past them.

"Some shit is getting ready to kick off," said John.

Some Mexicans standing in and near the weight pen signaled others who were working out on the weights. They stopped working out and lifted barbells into their hands as they stood around the weight pen. Some of the Aryan Brothers stepped up on the bleachers so they could be over top of the Mexicans. The other Aryan Brothers walked straight toward the Mexicans. The Mexicans started pulling their shanks out as the Aryan Brothers got closer.

The Aryan Brothers snatched out their shanks. Some of the Aryan's shanks were as long as lawnmower blades. When the Aryan Brothers came closer, Devil yelled, "Go!"

The Aryan Brothers, who were on top of the bleachers, jumped down on top of the Mexicans with knives in hands. The other Aryan Brothers ran over to the war. Some of the Mexicans swung barbells, knives, and weight poles. Blood splashed everywhere as flesh was being ripped apart. Some of the men screamed out in pain. A lot of the men fell to the ground only to be stabbed or poled viciously. The guards sounded off the loud horns and started shooting at the fight. Men fell from being shot; others fell from knives and pole clubbing. Once the guards had everything under control, all of the inmates laid on the ground; five of the men were dead. The guards locked up the Aryan brothers and the Mexicans. The Dewitt truck came to get the dead. The prison went on lockdown until the next day.

Chapter Ten

When the cell doors opened, Sherman along with about a hundred other inmates walked onto the tier. Sherman walked back into his cell to grab his knife from under the bottom of his locker. Once he retrieved the knife and tucked it away in his waist, he walked back onto the tier. He walked upstairs to Brace's cell. The cell had a red curtain covering the bars so no one could see inside of it.

Sherman walked over to the cell and spoke, "Brace! Brace! Are you up?"

Brace spoke in an out of breath voice, "Sherm, I have company."

Sherman heard Diamond whisper.

"Who's that?" Diamond asked.

"That's Sherman, that's the one who you will be going in the visiting room with."

"Oh!" Diamond replied.

"Sherm, are you still out there!?" asked Brace.

"Yea, what's up?" Sherman replied.

"I'll be out in a little while!" Brace said.

Sherman said, "R-right."

Sherman walked down stairs to John's cell. John was washing his face at the mirror. He saw Sherman's reflection in the mirror then he turned to look at him.

"What's up, Playa?" asked John.

Sherman leaned his back on the wall and held his right hand on the bars.

"Nothing much."

Gangster walked up beside Sherman.

"What's up, fellas?"

"Nothing much, killer..." said John. "Sherman, did you go down and wake up Brace?"

"Yea, but Brace wasn't sleep. He has company."

John and Gangster just shook their heads in displeasure.

"Man, that dude has gone mad," said Gangster.

"So, what shall we do today?" asked Sherman.

Sherman heard his name being called over the intercom.

"What the fuck they want with me?" asked Sherman, "Ella isn't off work yet, so I know I don't have a visit."

"No telling what these people want," said John.

"Well, fellas," said Sherman, "I'll be back."

Sherman walked out of the cell. He looked up the tier and saw Brace and Diamond walking down the tier. Brace was carrying a wash cloth, a soap dish, shampoo, and had a towel on his shoulder. They stopped at Diamond's cell. Diamond disappeared in his cell after giving Brace a hug.

Brace yelled to Sherman, "What's up, Sherm!?"

"I'm getting ready to go to The Bubble!"

"R-right! Hey!" Brace called out to Sherman.

Sherman turned back around and looked at him.

"Yea?"

"Tell John and Gangster, I'm getting ready to get in the shower. I need them to watch my back!"

Sherman nodded his head in agreement. He then walked back over to John's cell. Gangster was standing in the doorway.

"Damn, that was fast," said Gangster

"I didn't go down there yet," said Sherman. "Brace is trying to get in the shower. He wants y'all to watch his back."

John had put his face rag away and he turned toward his cell door.

"R-right."

Sherman walked down to the Bubble while John and Gangster walked down to Brace's cell. Sherman stood in front of The Bubble's window.

Corporal Kritz walked over to the window and pushed the intercom button.

"Are you Sherman Ford?" asked Corporal Kritz.

"Yeah."

"You have to go to the medical unit. Grab your pass out of the slot." Corporal Kritz ordered.

"I don't know where the medical unit is," Sherman responded.

"Once you get through the two gates, it's the second door on the right!" Corporal Kritz informed.

"R-right," said Sherman.

Corporal Kritz walked away from the window. Sherman went and pulled the pass out of the slot and walked over to the gate. The gate slid open, he walked through to the second gate. The first one closed and the second one opened. Sherman proceeded to the door that read, "Medical Unit." The first thing he saw was a long hallway. He walked ten feet pass a wall and saw Nurse Rebecca and Jackie in a small room. Both women were Black. Jackie was typing. Nurse Rebecca was leaning against one of the two lockers, while talking to Jackie. Sherman heard a male's voice say, "Hey!" He looked to the right where he heard the voice coming from. He spotted Corporal Hicks, a medium built white guard sitting in a chair that was up against the wall.

"Come here," Corporal Hicks said.

Corporal Hicks was about eleven steps away from him. Sherman started walking toward the man. He looked to his right and saw about eight other inmates sitting in chairs in a small waiting room. He noticed health pictures on the walls. He then glanced to the left. Nurse Rebecca smiled at him. He acknowledged her by nodding his head. Once he was standing in front of the officer, he saw Nurse Rose, a white woman physician walk into a small examination room and close the door behind her.

Sherman looked Corporal Hicks in his eyes, "Yea! What do you want?"

"Do you have a pass to be in here," asked Corporal Hicks?"

Sherman handed the pass to Corporal Hicks.

Corporal Hicks stood up, "Follow me, you belong in the other waiting room."

Sherman and Corporal Hicks walked over to the waiting room. The guard stuck a key in the door and pushed it open.

One of the inmates in the room ran to the door, "Man, I've been in here two hours! They haven't called me yet!"

"They will get to you in a minute," said Corporal Hicks, "Now step back so this man can get in."

The inmate sized Sherman up before he moved out of his path. Sherman then walked in the room. Corporal Hicks pulled the door closed. The inmate who was at the door, called the guard a bitch before he sat down. Corporal Hicks didn't hear the man because of the fiberglass window. Sherman sat down on the far end of the bench. Palmer, a frail,

141

sickly looking, older man was seated in a wheelchair leaning back with his eyes closed next to Sherman.

Palmer opened his eyes and spoke in a weak voice, "What's up, Playa?"

"Ain't shit," said Sherman.

"You just got here," asked Palmer.

"Yea. Why?" Sherman said sternly.

"Just take my advice, do not mess with the boys who are running around here posing as women." Palmer warned.

"Slim, check this out, I don't fuck around like that so you don't even have to tell me no shit like that!" Sherman barked.

"Nah, Playa, I didn't mean to disrespect you. I just wanted to put you down." Palmer said in a reassuring tone.

"Well, thanks for the advice. Sherman's voice was still sharp and mean."

"Playa, those bitches gave me the AIDS virus. I just wanted to look out for you. Playa, this shit is no joke. I'm dying a painful death. My body doesn't even obey me anymore." Palmer confided.

Sherman eased up. He felt sorry for the man.

"Damn, Slim." Sherman replied.

"Playa, don't feel sorry for me. I had no right making love to another man. I'm sorry that I am

142

dying but there is nothing anyone can do to stop this process. They have been giving me this medicine to slow up the process, but I am dying," Palmer said confidently, "Playa, I will be glad when death does come. I am living in constant pain."

"Man, I would have killed the motherfucker who gave it to me." Sherman barked.

"I didn't. I hear the bitch is still healthy as shit, but I'm dying. I wish I would have killed the bitch now. I'm lying around in the hospital now, I can't even walk. This shit has deteriorated my leg muscles. I'm going blind and this bitch is still in population fucking." Palmer disclosed with displeasure.

"Yea?" Sherman replied.

"Yup, you may have seen the tall skinny, red bitch? His name is Diamond," Palmer said as he looked at Sherman with one eye open.

Sherman was astonished, "What!?"

Sherman jumped to his feet. The man became scared. Sherman spoke with anger in his voice.

"What did you say that bitch name is!?" He demanded.

Palmer was shaking like a leaf. He started stuttering, "D-D-D-iamond."

"That bitch was with one of my buddies today!" Sherman said with irritation.

"Do you think he fucked him?" Palmer asked as he opened his other eye and turned slightly in Sherman's direction.

Sherman was furious.

"I know he fucked him! I'm going to kill that bitch!"

All of the other inmates were looking at him in surprise. Then Susan from the property room opened the door.

"Mr. Ford, would you please come here?" she asked.

The inmate who had come to the door when Sherman entered the room jumped up and ran over to Susan.

"I'm next!! Bitch, I'm next," said the inmate.

Susan became frightened. Sherman walked behind the man and spoke in a threatening voice.

"Bitch, you better get the fuck out of her face!" Sherman barked.

The man spun around and looked Sherman in his killer eyes. The man could see how serious Sherman was.

"Bitch," snarled Sherman, "I dare you! I dare you to move or to say anything!"

The man did not say a word. He just looked at Sherman. He knew Sherman would probably kill him right there and the guard wouldn't do anything because he just disrespected her. Sherman tossed the man to the wall and just looked at him. The man did not say anything. He just went and sat back down on the bench. Sherman turned to Susan.

"Yes Ma'am?" He said, smiling.

Susan smiled up at Sherman.

"Would you please step out here?" she requested.

Susan stepped aside and Sherman walked past her. She closed the door and locked it.

"Thanks for sticking up for me." she said, blushing.

Sherman didn't respond, he just looked at her.

"What's wrong?" asked Susan.

"Nothing."

Susan knew she wouldn't get the truth out of him so she changed the subject.

"I will be working up here tonight. Sooo… I will be calling you up here, okay?" she said, girlishly.

"For what?" he said with no emotions.

Susan smiled up at him," So, we can talk." she said as she swayed.

Sherman knew what she wanted and he planned to give it to her. He started smiling. "Now there's that smile I love," said Susan.

"So is that thing easy to get wet?" he replied.

Susan licked her lips, "You bet. You will get to see it drip."

Sherman's smile became brighter, "I can't wait."

"It won't be too much longer but it's well worth the wait." she smiled.

"So what's in it for me?" asked Sherman.

"Anything your heart desires." she batted her eyes.

"Well, my heart desires a lot." he smirked.

"I think I can take care of that, too," Susan said smiling.

"We will see." he said.

Susan started rocking the top of her body side to side.

"We will see."

Nurse Rose came out of the examination room. An inmate followed behind her.

"Send me another one," she said.

"Go ahead, Mr. Ford," said Susan. "I have to lock this other man in the holding pen."

Sherman nodded his head and walked into the doctor's room. When he came out, Susan sent him back to his unit. He saw his friends weren't in their cells, so he went into his cell and covered his hand with plastic so that nothing could get on them. He grabbed a mask and walked to the recreation room door. He put the mask over his face, pulled out

146

his knife and walked into the recreation room. Every man's eyes in the room bulged when they saw him enter the room.

Some of the men leaped back or up and snatched out their knives; even John, Gangster, and Brace leaped to their feet and pulled their knives out. Sherman glanced around the room. He spotted his prey sitting in a chair with his back turned to him. Diamond was too busy boasting loudly that he didn't even notice that a masked man had entered the room. Sherman walked up behind him and stabbed him viciously in the neck, top of the head and back. Diamond was only able to let out one muffled scream. The blow to the head killed him instantly. His body slumped to the floor after his head crashed into the table he was seated at. As soon as the body hit the floor, Sherman started kicking the bloody corpse. Brace was about to charge Sherman but John grabbed him by the arm.

"That's Sherman," John whispered.

Brace looked at John in disbelief. Sherman left the room without taking off his mask until he got on the other side of the door. He went into his cell and flushed the plastic down the toilet, cleaned his knife and hid it in its hiding place. John, Gangster and Brace walked into his cell. Brace looked furious. Sherman was looking up at the men from his relaxed position in his bed.

"Why the fuck did you do that!?" asked Brace.

Sherman stood up and looked Brace straight in the eyes.

"That bitch gave you a death sentence," said Sherman.

"What the fuck are you talking about!?" Brace demanded.

"That bitch has the AIDS virus!" Sherman shouted.

All of them looked shocked.

"What the fuck are you talking about?" repeated Brace.

Brace's facial expression had changed.

"Brace," said Sherman, "man that bitch got the bug and [13]she has given it to you."

"Man, you don't know what the fuck you are talking about!" Brace barked.

"Man, I just got finished talking to a motherfucker she gave it to!" Sherman informed.

Sherman could tell Brace believed him but he tried to deny it by making a joke.

"Well, I have to die from something." Brace snickered

Brace walked to the door and he looked back at Sherman.

"Thanks, Playa." Brace said with sadness in his voice.

Brace walked off.

---

[13] Some m*en in prison call homosexuals 'her' and 'she' because that is what they prefer to be called.*

"Damn!" exclaimed John.

"That is fucked up," said Gangster.

"That is why I killed that bitch!" said Sherman.

"I know he feels fucked up right now," said Gangster.

Sherman stood up and brushed his hands across his pants legs.

"Look, I'm going down to talk to him," said Sherman.

"We're going with you," said John.

The three men walked upstairs to Brace's cell. Brace had his shirt off and was shadow boxing in the mirror. He saw them in the mirror but continued shadow boxing while he spoke to them.

"Come on in."

The three men stepped inside of the cell. Brace threw two left jabs and a right hook in front of the mirror. Then he started bouncing up and down in place.

"What's up?" asked Brace.

Brace glanced over at them and then he looked back at the mirror still bouncing.

"I'm sorry, Playa," said Sherman, apologetically.

"Don't trip, we all have to die of something. I am still in good shape, maybe the dude who told you that was wrong," said Brace.

"Go get yourself tested to make sure," said John.

Brace glanced over at John.

"Man, fuck that!" said Brace, still bouncing.   I don't want to know if I got that shit, I want it to just kill me."

A crowd of guards walked to the cell. Corporal James hit the bars with his club.

"Emergency lockdown! Let's go!" he shouted.

The four men knew it was because of Diamond's death. The three men exited the cell and were locked in their cell. Sherman laid down and went to sleep.

Chapter Eleven

Sherman was lying on his bed asleep facing the wall under his window. He woke up and rolled over when he heard the loud man's voice on the intercom.

"Ford!" shouted Corporal James.

Sherman spoke still half asleep.

"What?"

"You have a visitor, come to the booth and get your pass!" Corporal James said, still shouting.

"R-right!"

Sherman sat up in bed and swung his feet around onto the floor. He stood up and walked over to his locker, grabbed his washcloth, toothbrush, and toothpaste out of the locker. He then walked over to the sink, washed his face and brushed his teeth. He changed into his prison outfit in order to go to the visiting room. He put on his thick coat with a fur hood. He saw through his window that it was raining outside. Sherman's cell door slid open, he walked onto the tier. The tier was empty. He turned and walked to John's cell. John was lying on his back watching his television on the desk. John looked at the door when a shadow came over him. When he saw it was Sherman, he stood up and walked over to the bars.

"What's up, Sherm," asked John, "What are you doing out?"

"They just called me for a visit." Sherman replied.

"So, are you going up there to pick that up?" John questioned.

"Yea." Sherman replied.

"I'll see you when you get back then." John said and returned his focus to the television.

"R-right." Sherman replied.

Sherman walked upstairs to Brace's cell. Brace was still asleep so Sherman walked over to Gangster's cell. Gangster was sitting in a chair watching television. He quickly turned his head when he sensed someone at his cell door. Sherman was smiling at him. Gangster got up and walked over to the bars smiling.

"What's up, young Gangster?" asked Sherman.

"Just watching Oprah... We're still on lockdown, what are you doing out?" Gangster replied.

"I'm getting ready to go on a visit." Sherman informed him

"Oh!" Gangster said with excitement.

"How is your girl doing?" asked Sherman.

"She's still on the machine. They already said the baby is dead," said Gangster. "They still don't know if my girl is going to pull through. Man, we can have another baby. I just want her to live."

"I can understand that," said Sherman. "She's going to pull through, and you're right. Y'all will have another child. Maybe, ya will have a little mob."

Gangster started smiling, and then his face got kind of serious.

"Oh yea! Chop wrote me and told me KT is also on a machine." Gangster said as he slowly slipped into sadness.

"What!?" exclaimed Sherman. "What happened!?"

"Some bama stabbed him up while he was asleep." Gangster said as he shook his head in regret.

"Damn!" said Sherman.

"Chop also said the dude got sent up here." Gangster said with a smirk.

"Did he say the dude's name?" Sherman asked, eagerly.

"Yea, the dude's name is Oliver Mills." Gangster said as he gripped the bars with his hands.

"If he is here, we will find him and destroy his bitch ass." Sherman barked.

"That's what I had in mind," said Gangster.

"Look, I will talk to you when I get back," said Sherman.

"R-right."

Sherman went to The Bubble and got the pass. He went to the visiting room. The visiting room was crowded with inmates and their families. When Sherman walked through the door, an admiring female watched him walk all the way to the table and sit down in a chair. When Sherman sat down, he looked back to see if the very pretty brown skin woman was still watching him, which she was. He smiled and waved at the woman. She waved back at Sherman. Then she blew him a kiss. He started blushing and turned around.

When Sherman turned around he saw Ella walk through the visiting room doors. He stood up when Ella got close to him. They hugged and kissed. As they were kissing, Ella used her tongue to push the balloon into Sherman's mouth. His eyes had bulged because, for a moment, he had forgotten about what he had asked Ella to do. When he pulled away from her, he started smiling. Then they both sat down. Sherman looked back over to the woman who blew him a kiss. She rolled her eyes at him and turned her head. Sherman turned around to face Ella.

"What is wrong?" Ella asked.

"Nothing. Why do you ask?" he said..

"Because you were looking around the room." she replied.

"I thought I saw somebody I knew." he said.

"Oh."
"So, how is everything?" Sherman asked.

"Everything is fine, I'm just tired. I worked hard today." Ella said in exhaustion.

Sherman pushed the balloon to the side of his mouth so that he could talk better.

"I am not going to keep you here long. How is Loretta doing?" he asked.

"The same. She is just steady getting big." Ella said, smiling proudly.

"Yea?" he said, smiling.

"Yup, Boo, you look like you are getting small. Are you worrying?" Ella said with a look of concern.

Sherman started laughing, "Nah! They just feed us like chickens in here. Plus, the food taste like shit."

"You better start eating it." she warned.

Sherman didn't say anything because he carefully watched three hoodlums, who just walked through the visiting room doors, to visit an inmate. He kept his eyes on them as they went to the table behind him. There was a medium build, fair skinned man standing up in front of the table. The three men hugged and shook the man's hand. Then they all sat down at the table. Sherman turned back around to look at Ella. He heard one of the men say, "Oliver." Sherman looked back around toward the men. One of the men started talking to their friend.

"Oliver, man, these people act like they weren't going to let us in," said the first man.

"Why wasn't they?" asked Oliver.

"They were saying," the second man began to answer, "that there is no Oliver Mills on The Hill." I said, "He just came on The Hill 'cause he stabbed somebody up. The broad called down to your unit and she said, 'He is here. He just went into cell one.' Then she let us in."

Ella tapped Sherman on his hand. He turned around to face Ella. She looked worried.

"What's wrong, Baby?" Ella questioned.

"Nothing, Baby." he said.

Sherman held up one finger "Hold on for one minute, Ella."

Ella remained quiet while Sherman continued to eavesdrop on the conversation Oliver and his friends were engaged in.

"Did the bama you stabbed up die yet?" asked the third man.

Oliver spoke in a bragging tone of voice.

"Nah," said Oliver, "but my youngens got that. I don't think the fool is going to live anyway. They have him hooked up to a machine. I stabbed the fool in his head, back and all over his body. All the bitch nigga did was kept trying to grab for his knife until his bitch ass went unconscious."

Sherman smiled at the thought of KT trying to get his knife to fight back. When Sherman looked at Oliver and his friends, he was filled with hatred for the four men.

Ella spoke again, "Boo, turn around."

Oliver heard Ella telling Sherman to turn around. When Oliver looked over in the direction of

*Ella's voice, he looked Sherman straight in his eyes.
Sherman gave Oliver a wicked smile, and then he
turned back around.*

"What's wrong, Baby?" Ella asked Sherman.

"Nothing. I'm sorry. I was just trying to hear
something I needed to hear." he said, apologetically.

"And what was that?" she inquired.

"Nothing of any importance to you." he reassured
her.

"Do you need anything else?" she said as she tried to
read his eyes.

"No." he said as he looked down at the table.

"Oh yea, Ed said if you need some more just let him
know." she said with excitement.

"Okay. I want you to tell him that he will bring it
down next time. You are not doing this anymore."
Sherman stated.

"Okay." she said, relieved.

Sherman grabbed her hands and stood up.

"Look Boo, you go ahead home and get yourself
some rest. I will call you soon, and give Loretta a
kiss for me, okay?"

"Okay, give me a kiss." She said before she leaned in
to receive a kiss.

"I can't give you a kiss unless you're carrying this
shit back with you?" Sherman said, smiling.

157

Ella knew he was playing.

"Sheeed! I was scared to death coming in here." she said, smiling.

Sherman smiled and pulled her to him and gave her a peck on her lips.

"I love you," said Sherman.

"I love you, too."

"I'm going to call you, okay?" he said.

"Okay, I want you to start eating," Ella pleaded.

Sherman said smiling, "Yea, whatever."

She burst into laughter. Then she grabbed his face and kissed his forehead before swaying her hips as she exited the visiting room. Sherman followed the guard into the back of the visiting room. He became frightened when the guard told him to take off his clothes. He thought the guard was going to tell him to open his mouth but he didn't.

He walked back down to his building. No one was on the tier. He ran up the steps to Gangster's cell. Gangster was watching television.

"Gangster!" yelled Sherman.

Gangster turned around to see that his friend stood at the bars. He walked over to the bars.

"How was your visit?" asked Gangster.

"Better than you will believe." Sherman said with excitement.

Both of the men smiled.

"What happened?" Gangster eagerly said.

"I saw Oliver." Sherman whispered.

"What!?" Gangster shouted.

"Yea, some of his buddies came to see him. One of them said his whole name. Then Oliver started bragging about stabbing KT. The bitch nigga said KT kept grabbing for his knife until he was unconscious." Sherman informed him.

Gangster giggled and shook his fist in the air.

"That's my nigga! He's a soldier until the end." Gangster said, bragging.

"Yea, dude sleeps in cell one, across from The Bubble." Sherman said.

"It doesn't make a difference. He is dead when the door pops!" Gangster said as he paced in front of his cell door.

"It does make a difference. We don't have long here and we're not going to run our bits up. We'll get him though." Sherman said.

Gangster started nodding his head, "R-right, I just want to kill the chump."

"We got that. Whenever the doors pop, come down to my cell."

"R-right."

Sherman had started walking away, and then Gangster called him back to his cell.

"What's up?" asked Sherman.

"Did you get that?"

"Yea, I got that in my pocket." Sherman replied.

Gangster's smile widens.

"R-right."

Sherman hit Gangster's cell door with his hand.

"It's going to be all right."

Gangster nodded his head. Sherman walked to his cell and went inside of it. Sherman stopped by Brace's and John's cell but both of them were asleep, so he went to his cell.

He sat down and removed the razor blade from one of his shaving razors. He used the blade to chop the crack cocaine into small pieces, on top of his desk. Corporal James' voice came over the intercom.

"Ford!" said Corporal James.

Sherman jumped up. He thought he had gotten caught with drugs but when he didn't see anyone at the bars, he knew it was the intercom. "What!?"

"You have a medical pass!" said Corporal James.

"R-right."

>*Sherman put the cocaine back into the balloon and tied a string around the top of the balloon. Then he shoved his hand down the toilet drain and rigged the balloon against a snag in the pipe. The bare end of the string was visible in the water. Whenever he needs to retrieve the drugs, he'll just pull on the string.*

>*Sherman walked out of his cell, picked up the pass and walked into the medical unit. Susan was leaning on the wall. When she saw him, she started smiling. Sherman walked over to her and stood in front of her.*

"What's up?" he said in a lustful tone.

"What took you so long?" she said as she gently poked him in the chest.

"The guards took long to open the cell." he confided.

"Oh, I called for you earlier. They said you were gone on a visit." she said with a smirk.

"I was."

"Did you enjoy your visit?" she said with envy.

"Sure did." he replied.

"Who came to see you?" she said as she poked him again in his chest.

"That's irrelevant." he grabbed her finger, locked eyes with her, and gently put her hand to her side.

"I'm sorry for prying." she said with an innocent expression.

"Don't worry about that. So what's up with you?" Sherman said, smiling.

Susan looked around and she didn't see anybody so she ran her hand between his legs and licked her lips.

"You!" she said smiling.

Sherman smiled.

"I like that." he said.

She ran her hands between her legs. "Then you will love this." she said as she bit down on her bottom lip.

"Must be nice." he said.

"I am, believe me." she said.

"I'm not interested in all this talking, I'm ready to fuck." he said, impatiently.

"Well, follow me then." she said.

"Lead the way!" he said, grinning.

Sherman followed her down the long hallway. She opened the room door storage closet and turned on the lights. The room was full of shelves with white sheets and gowns. There was a stretcher against the wall.

She gestured for him to enter. Once he was inside, she kissed him, and then she pulled herself

*away. She sat on top of the stretcher as he walked in
between her legs, he kissed her passionately. She
laid back as she begun unbuttoning her shirt, and
revealing her firm white breasts with erect pink
nipples. She licked the tip of her finger and circled
her left nipple.*

"Aah! Aah! Fuck me, Mr. Ford!" she ordered. "Fuck
me right now."

*She removed her pants. She wore black lace
panties. The panties came off. Her pubic hairs
barely hid her thick lips. He was just staring at her
firm naked body. She sat up and faced him. She
planted the bottom of her feet on the stretcher and
opened her legs. Her opening parted for him. She
started caressing her clitoris.*

"Aah! Aah! Oooh my God, please put that dick in
me."

He smiled before slowly sliding his pants
below his knees. Her eyes widen with desire as his
erection swayed before her without him touching it.
He made his way over to her and inserted the tip of
his erection inside of her.

"O GOD!!" Susan screamed.

*She wrapped her arms around his neck and
eased herself to the end of his erection. Her closed
eyes tightened. Then she viciously bounced up and
down on his erection. He lifted and held her in the
air by her butt cheeks. She continued to ride him so
hard and fast that he had to place his back against
the wall to keep his balance. She continued bouncing
wildly and she began licking the side of his face.*

"Oh Mr Ford! Oh Mr. Ford. I'm cumming!! I'm cumming!!" panted Susan.

She began bouncing up and down on him even harder. Her eyes seemed to be rolling in the back of her head when she was having her orgasm, she then looked Sherman straight in the eyes.

"Let me down. Please fuck me now…"

Sherman put her down. She walked over to one of the shelves and grabbed hold of it with both hands and bent over until her pubic was visible in between her ass cheeks. He stepped up behind her, gripped the rack above him with one hand, and eased his erection halfway inside of her pussy. He eased the tip of his finger in her ass then he began to thrust his erection all the way inside of her. She sighed and started gyrating her hips. He gripped her waist with both hands and began pounding inside of her. She screamed in full enjoyment. Once he came, he pulled out of her and pulled up his pants. She turned to face him. She looked tired as she ran her hand through her hair and let out a deep breath.

"That was wonderful. I think you made me bleed," she said with a huge smile on her face.

"I thought that's what I saw too. I saw a little blood on the tip of my shit." he replied.

"I most likely will be sore tomorrow. I've never been fucked like that. What size is that big ass dick of yours, nineteen and an half inches?"

Sherman started laughing.

"You are a crazy white broad."

Susan was smiling.

"You liked it." she asked with a serious look.

Sherman just laughed.

"I work in here all this week and next week and I'm going to call you up here every night, okay?" she cooed.

"Cool with me." he replied.

Susan looked at Sherman seriously.

"Sherman, I never fucked an inmate or black guy before, I think I love you though." she confided.

"That's nice." he replied.

Susan got dressed. Sherman went back to his cell and washed up. Then he turned off the light and went to sleep.

Chapter Twelve

When the cell doors opened, Sherman woke up. He pushed his body erect by using his hands and sat on the edge of his bed with hands wrapped around the top of his head. He looked over at the sunlight coming through his window. Then he did his morning routine of taking a piss and grabbing his hygiene items. While he was brushing his teeth, Gangster came into his cell. Sherman looked at his friend from the mirror and nodded his head. Then he rinsed his mouth and spat into the toilet before he turned to face his friend.

"What's up, asked Sherman?"

"I just came past that nigga, Oliver's cell. That nigga is still asleep. I was going to kill him in his sleep but the guards would have seen me going in." Gangster said with a look of irritation.

Sherman put on his clothes while he talked.

"I told you that yesterday."

"We have to get this nigga!" Gangster said as he started pacing.

"We're going to get him. Let's go down to John's cell and tell him what's up." Sherman suggested.

Both men walked down to John's cell. John was in his cell doing push-ups.

"…415, 416, 417…" counted John.

Sherman laughed out loud.

"Joker, stop lying to yourself!" said Sherman.

John let his body drop to the floor.

"Let's help his crazy ass up!" said Sherman. "He probably can't get up on his own."

Gangster grabbed one of John's arms and Sherman grabbed the other. They pulled him to his feet. John sat down on the edge of his unmade bed. He was letting out deep breaths. Sherman was still laughing.

"You're a fake dude," said Sherman. "You probably saw us coming down here then you decided to put on a little show for us. You are a fake dude, you know."

"Sheeed," said John, "I'm in perfect shape."

"Sheeed!" said Sherman. "You have a body like an old pair of shoes. You're all fucked up!"

They all busted out into laughter.

"So what's up," asked John. "You said you had to holla at me about something important."

"Yea, this dude stabbed up KT," said Sherman.

John jumped to his feet "What!? Is he all right?" he demanded.

"Chop said he is living off of a breathing machine," said Gangster.

John shook his head, "Damn!! That is my youngen! Did Chop and them torture the motherfucka!?"

"Nah," said Gangster, "that's our job."

"What!?" asked John.

"The bama is on The Hill with us," said Sherman.

"What?" John was still surprised. "Where he at!?"

"Cell one," Gangster said.

John lifted up his bed. There were five knives under his bed, they were all different sizes. He grabbed the longest knife. The knife was sixteen inches long. He turned around towards his friends. Their eyes showed their astonishment.

"Let's go!" said John.

"Good God O'Mighty!" exclaimed Gangster, "Where the fuck did you get that!?"

"Fuck that!" said John. "Let's go get this chump motherfucka!"

"Hold tight, John," said Sherman.

John looked at Sherman in disbelief, "What!?"

"The man sleeps in cell one," said Sherman.

"I don't give a fuck!" John said.

"John, listen up, man," Sherman said, "The Bubble is right across from his cell."

"And," John said with irritation.

168

"We can't get him without catching another charge," Sherman explained.

Brace walked in John's cell and he saw the knife in John's grip.

"What the fuck is going on with ya'll?" asked Brace.

They all looked at Brace.

"The chump that's in cell one? He's the motherfucker that stabbed one of my little henchmen," John snapped.

"You just can't run up in there," said Brace. "The guards are right across from there... Look, check this out, I'm going to get some people to distract the guards then only two of you can go up in the cell."

"That sounds good," said Sherman. "Do that."

Brace walked out of the cell.

"I'm going in! All of us can't go in like he said," John said.

"All I know is Gangster is going in!" said Gangster.

"R-right," said Sherman. "Y'all two go in, I'll stay outside of the cell."

Brace walked back into the cell, "I got the distraction, remember only two can go in."

"John and Gangster are going in," Sherman said to Brace.

"R-right. Me and you will stand outside of the cell. Let's go." Brace said.

The four men walked out of the cell and headed to Oliver's cell. They saw Corporal James, Corporal Kritz, and Corporal Hicks trying to control a heated argument between five homosexuals. Brace signaled his friends to stop.

"Let me walk on past the cell to see if he is asleep or what. We don't need to hear no hollering, so y'all have to do this right."

They all nodded their heads in agreement with him. Then they all started walking down to the cell. John, Sherman, and Gangster stopped at cell two while Brace kept on walking. Sherman looked in the cell. There was an inmate in there lying on his bed, writing a letter. He looked up and spotted them. He was instantly consumed with the fear of losing his life.

Brace walked past Oliver's cell. Oliver was seated on his bed and reading the newspaper. He never looked up to see Brace. Brace walked past and leaned against the wall by Oliver's cell. He then glanced over at the guards, who were still trying to gain control of the argument. Brace looked at his friends. He signaled a thumbs up in the air to let them know Oliver was awake. He then simulated someone reading a newspaper. John shook his head that he understood.

Gangster snatched out his knife and hid it by his leg as he entered the cell first. Oliver noticed the knife before he spotted who was holding it. John stepped in beside Gangster. Oliver was immediately struck with fear. The newspaper dropped to the floor. He sprung to his feet, not really knowing what he

170

would do next. *Gangster stared the man straight in his eyes. Oliver could see the hatred Gangster had for him in his eyes.*

"This is for KT!" growled Gangster.

Gangster plunged toward Oliver. Oliver charged Gangster empty handed. Gangster stabbed him in his chest. Oliver's eyes opened wide, in total shock. Oliver then grabbed Gangster around his arms, trying to hold the knife away from stabbing him. Gangster was strong and fast. He continued pushing the knife through the man's flesh. Oliver desperately sunk his teeth deep into Gangster's shoulder.

Gangster yelled out in agony, "Aahh! This bitch is biting me!! Ahhh!"

Brace and Sherman looked at each other also in shock before they looked over to the guards. The guards were too engaged in the arguing and didn't seem aware of the screams.

"See what the fuck is going on in there!" Brace told Sherman.

Sherman peeped in the room. He saw that John had jammed his knife halfway into Oliver's back. Then with force, he ripped the knife up his back in the direction of his shoulder. Oliver's head titled back and his arms uncontrollably shot up into the air. Gangster viciously started stabbing him in his chest. Oliver's knees buckled and he collapsed to the floor. John snatched his knife free. Gangster bends over the body and started stabbing Oliver in his head. John forcefully pulled Gangster away from Oliver. John looked into Gangster's eyes and saw his rage.

171

"Gangster, Gangster, calm down!" soothed John.

Gangster shook his head trying to regain control of himself.

He then looked at John's face and spoke, "I'm okay."

"Let's go," said John.

As they started to exit the cell, Corporal Hicks approached, and saw the dead body. Sherman immediately thrust one of his arms around Corporal Hicks' neck, choking him, and began rapidly stabbing him in the back as he forced him into the cell. The guard's eyes rolled in the back of his head. John raised his palm and signaled Sherman to stop, which he did after stabbing him one more time. Then he let the corpse fall to the floor. He turned around and walked out of the cell and his friends followed behind him. They all went into their cells, cleaned themselves, washed off their knives, and stashed the weapons.

The prison guards did a search of the cells for the missing guard. They discovered him and the other dead man in cell one. They called for backup and immediately locked the prison down. The guards ransacked every cell in the prison. They locked up eighteen men and recovered sixty-four knives and other contraband. However, they didn't discover any weapons in Sherman's cell or the cells of his friends. After the search, the prison was kept on lockdown.

A few hours later, Gangster walked to Sherman's cell. Sherman lay on his back reading a novel. Gangster tapped on the bars with his hand. Sherman walked over to the bars once he saw him there.

"What's up? What are you doing out?" Sherman asked as he tried to peer down the tier.

"I have an emergency phone call," said Gangster.

Sherman said smiling, "Maybe it's something good." "I doubt it; I just hope my girl is alright."

Gangster sounded sad.

"It's probably her making the call. Ella did that before just to talk to me." Sherman said, smiling

"I hope so." Gangster whispered.

"It's going to be all right. Holla at me when you get back, r-right." Sherman cheerfully replied.

"R-right."

Gangster walked on down the tier. Sherman went and sat down on the edge of his bed. He picked up his book and started reading it again. Fifteen minutes later, Gangster was standing in front of Sherman's cell, tapping lightly on the bars. Sherman sat the book down on his bed and walked over to the bars. Gangster was avoiding making eye contact by looking down at the floor.

He spoke in a soft gentle voice, "What's up, Gangster? Who was it?"

Gangster had his head down then he looked up at Sherman with tears running down his face.

"She died on me." Gangster mumbled.

Tears poured down Gangster's face and he sniffed trying to hold back his tears but he didn't wipe them away.

Gangster repeated "She died on me, Sherm."

Sherman felt so sorry for his friend, but he knew nothing he could say would change the way his friend felt. The weather even changed to the occasion. It thundered and lightened outside. Sherman tried to comfort his friend with gentle words.

"Gangster, you're going to be all right." Sherman proclaimed.

Gangster shouted back, "Not without her! She was my life! No one else cared about me! She was the only one there for me!"

Gangster lowered his head and put his hands in his pockets.

"Now she's gone." Gangster mumbled.

"Gangster, you're a strong man. You have to pull through this. I know you loved her but you are going to have to put this behind you. You must go on with your life."

Gangster looked back up at his friend and spoke in a soft voice.

"You don't understand, Sherm. She was my life. Nothing else mattered to me but her."

"I understand Gangster, Man, we are both still young. You will meet other women."

Gangster shouted back at Sherman, "I don't want anyone else! She is all that I wanted and needed!!"

"Calm down, Playa. I know how you feel but she's gone now. She would want you to go on and enjoy life."

"How would you know!? You never knew her!" Gangster replied with contempt.

"If she loved you, like I believed she did, she would only want to see you happy." Sherman replied.

"She is dead, Sherman. Just like that! I didn't even get to hold her again and tell her I loved her." Gangster confessed

Gangster looked up to the ceiling, way up on the sixth floor.

"Damn!! Why God, I prayed to you but you didn't help her!" Gangster said with tears pouring from his eyes.

"Gangster, Gangster!" Sherman shouted.

Gangster looked back at his friend.

"She is okay now," said Sherman. "She ain't in any more pain. She's with God. She'll be watching over you now. So, you better get your shit together and make her proud. You didn't lose her. She'll always be with you. She knew you loved her. You know she didn't want to leave you, but God needed her with him."

Gangster looked at Sherman seriously. He had that same look in his eyes that John saw.

"Me and God are beefin'. He took my baby and my girl. Now I won't get to see either one of them again. It's on." Gangster said reassuringly.

"Gangster, you are talking crazy now," said Sherman. "Get a grip on yourself. You will get to see her again."

"How? She is dead! There is no coming back!" Gangster shouted as he began to pace.

"She will always be in your heart. You will see her every time you think about her. You will see her in her pictures, just like you see her right now. She will always be living in your thoughts. And when you die, God will put you both together. Gangster, you must live your life and look forward to seeing her when you die." Sherman professed.

Corporal James yelled through the intercom in Sherman's cell, *"Ramon Luket! Your cell has been popped open! Lock in now!!"*

Gangster shouted back, "Fuck you!!"

"Calm down," said Sherman. "Go ahead in your cell and we will talk when we come off lockdown."

"R-right." Gangster said as he nodded his head. "Gangster!" Sherman said.

Gangster looked back at Sherman "What's up?"

"We're family now. So, lock that in your brain; I'm your family. I love you like a brother, so be strong. We'll talk."

Gangster started smiling – "Okay, Bro."

Gangster walked off. An hour later, all of the cell doors opened. Sherman came out of his cell and walked up to Gangster's cell. His heart started racing when he saw Gangster's body dangling from the ceiling. He had hung himself with his television cord. Sherman ran in a rage and jumped up on top of the desk in Gangster's cell. Then he pulled out his knife. Brace and John had just walked to the cell and saw Gangster's body and ran into the cell. They grabbed his waist as Sherman had cut the cord. They laid him down on the bed. Sherman jumped down off of the desk. He was crying. He ran over to the body and started performing CPR on his friend.

Brace and John knew just as well as Sherman did that Gangster was dead. The extension cord had torn through his flesh and cut his windpipe. John tried to pull Sherman away from the body but Sherman yanked away from John's grip and continued to give the dead man CPR.

"He's dead, Sherman," John said.

Sherman pushed down on Gangster's chest trying to clear his lungs.

"No he isn't! Come on, Gangster! Come on! Don't die on me now! Come on!"

Brace and John grabbed Sherman and forcefully pulled him away from Gangster.

"The kid is dead!" said Brace. "There's nothing you can do!"

"Get off of me!! Get off of me!!" yelled Sherman.

"Sherman! Sherman! Calm down! Calm down!" shouted John.

Sherman cried again then he lowered his head and let the tears flow from his eyes. Brace and John were still holding his arms.

"Come on, Sherman," said John. "Let's carry his body down to The Bubble."

The two men picked up Gangster's dead body and carried it down to The Bubble. Brace followed close behind them. All of the other inmates stopped and watched the three men. One of the guards came running out of the booth. Sherman told him what happened and why he believed he killed himself. The guards locked everybody in except Sherman. The medics came and took the body away on the stretcher. The guards questioned Sherman then he went to his cell and thought about Gangster until he fell off to sleep.

Chapter Thirteen

Four and a half months later...

"Sherman! Get up," said Susan. "Get up, Sherman."

> *Sherman rolled over to see that Susan stood in front of his cell. She smiled over at him then she motioned her hand for him to come over to the bars.*

"Come and get this stuff," she said.

> *Susan waved him over with one hand and her other hand was between the bars showing him the white hard substance in a clear sandwich bag. Sherman rolled out of the bed and walked over to her and grabbed the bag. She grabbed his T-shirt with one of her hands and pulled him to the bars. She smiled as she spoke.*

"I love you and I believe I may be pregnant," she confided.

> *Sherman looked surprised.*

"You have been fucking me for the last 5 months. You didn't think I could become pregnant?" she asked.

Sherman rubbed his right hand over his head, "Damn."

"I was supposed to have come on my period last week. I don't even have any signs of me getting ready to come on." she confessed.

"You haven't been fucking with nobody else?" asked Sherman.

Susan was becoming mad.

"No! You have been the only dick I have been getting but you don't have to worry. I am not having the baby, if I am pregnant." she barked.

Susan walked away. Sherman started to call her back but decided not to. He walked over to his cell desk and emptied the cocaine onto the table. He walked over to his toilet and stood on top of it and started yelling Brace's name through the vent above the mirror.

"Hey Brace! Hey Brace! Hey Brace!" Sherman yelled.

"What!! Brace yelled back."

"I got that! You hear me!?" Sherman said, proudly.

"Yea! I'll be down when the doors open!" Brace replied.

"R-right!"

Sherman walked over to one of his lockers, tilted it to the side, and retrieved the razor blade from underneath the locker. Then he walked over to the table and started chopping the cocaine up in little pieces. He realized he didn't have any more bags to

*put them in so he went and stood back on top of the
toilet.*

"Hey Brace! Hey Brace!" Sherman shouted.

"What!?" Braced replied.

"I don't have any more plastic!" Sherman said.

"Fuck that shit! I don't have any more either!" Brace
said.

"Do you think John got some!?" Sherman
questioned.

"Nah! Fuck that shit though!" Brace said.

"R-right!" Sherman replied.

*Sherman jumped down and continued to
chop the cocaine up in little pieces. When the cell
doors popped, he was about finished. A few seconds
later, John and Brace walked into Sherman's cell. He
turned around to see who just entered his cell. When
he saw that it was only them, he turned around and
finished chopping. Both men came up and stood
behind him.*

"Slide me five of those joints, I have some buyers,"
said Brace.

*Sherman took the razor blade, and with it,
he slid five pieces of cocaine to the edge of the desk.
Brace picked up the pebble of cocaine and exited the
cell.*

"Your girl did count today," said John. "I know she
stopped by."

John was referring to Susan. Sherman spoke without turning his head to John.

"Yea, she dropped this off to me. Man, that ho' talking about she thinks she is pregnant." Sherman bragged.

John spoke in a toying voice, "W-h-a-t!"

"Man, that shit is not a joke. When I asked Susan was she fucking somebody else, she got mad and rolled out." Sherman said with a look and tone of disbelief.

"So if she's pregnant, that's her problem." John implied.

Sherman looked at his friend and shook his head, "Nah, John that is me *and* Susan's responsibility."

John was frowning as he spoke, "Man, I know you are not tripping off that ho'!"

"Nah, but if she is pregnant, that's my baby." Sherman replied, calmly.

John spoke in disbelief, "Man, you don't know that."

"She said she was only giving *me* the pussy." Sherman confessed.

"You don't know if that's the truth!" John barked.

"You're right and I don't know if it is not either." Sherman replied.

"So what about Ella?" John asked with a smirk.

"What do you mean, what about Ella?" Sherman replied.

"That is your l-i-v-i-n-g daughter's mother, what are you going to say, fuck her?" John asked.

"Nah, Fuck no!" Sherman snapped.

"Fuck that cracker!" said John. "I know how you feel thinking that baby maybe yours. But Sherman, you can't trip off that shit! She should've been on birth control."

Sherman just shook his head in disbelief.

"John, you are a cruddy dude... Anyway, she said 'she is not sure.' She just hasn't come on her period yet. And she said 'she was not going to have the baby anyway.'"

"Sherman, leave that cracker alone 'cause you're getting ready to get caught up in a lot of bullshit just because you have jungle fever." John smirked.

Both men laughed. Brace walked back into the cell and threw the money on the desk.

"Why you laughing?" asked Brace.

"You would not understand," said Sherman.

"Sherman," asked Brace, "did that skinny motherfucker Paul pay you for that coke I gave him?"

Sherman shook his head, "Nah."

"Let's go see this bitch!" said Brace.

Sherman stood up and grabbed one of his knives from under his bed, "Let's go!"

All three of the men left Sherman's cell. They walked up the steps to the second floor. The second floor tier was full with all races of inmates walking around. There were six white Aryan Brotherhood members who stood in front of the man's cell that Sherman and his friends were going to. Sherman and the others heard some loud screaming. All of the inmates on the tier started looking in the direction of the screaming. Sherman and his friends paused in the middle of the tier. They didn't want to walk into something they did not have anything to do with. The screaming and yelling continued for a few minutes. Devil and two other Aryan Brothers came carrying a small Mexican in the nude out of the cell, kicking and screaming. The men casually carried him right over to the rail and threw him over like a piece of paper. They leaned over the rail and watched as the man fell through the air screaming. Once the concrete silenced him, the Aryan Brothers stood up and laughed. Devil zipped up his pants. Then he noticed John, Sherman and Brace and nodded his head to them in a friendly gesture. Devil and his friends turned around and walked down the tier in the opposite direction of Sherman and his friends. Sherman and his friends immediately headed for the steps they came up. As they reached the steps, there were about twenty Mexicans running up the steps with knives in their hands. Sherman and his crew stepped aside. The Mexicans ran right past them. They turned and watched the Mexicans run down the tier.

"They're going to catch Devil and the rest of them Klansmen," said Brace.

"Devil raped that man, didn't he?" asked Sherman.

"Yup," said Brace.

"Well, their war is on again full blast, Sherman," said John.

"Let's go. The guards will be up here in full armor gear soon," said Brace.

They looked back down the hall and saw the two groups of men fighting. They turned around and walked down the steps.

"Sherman," said Brace, "Go hide that shit. They'll be doing a major shake down after they clean this shit up. Hide ya shanks, too. I am going"

Before Brace had the chance to finish his sentence, the prison horns sounded off. Brace pointed up to the second floor. Sherman had both of his hands over his ears.

"I will see you two in a couple of days!" Brace said.

Sherman and John both nodded their heads in agreement with Brace. Brace turned around and ran up the steps. As Sherman and John walked back to their cells, they passed three bloody bodies lying dead on the concrete. The men appeared to have been thrown off of the tier where the fight was. They both looked down the tier when they heard what sounded like a hundred footsteps. They saw the prison guards in full armor gear running up the stairs toward where the fighting was.

Some of the guards had shields, riot shotguns, clubs and they all wore helmets with shields over their faces. About twenty guards came running in the direction of the first floor tier. The guards were ordering all of the inmates on the tier to lie down on the floor. Sherman and John swiftly stepped into their cells and slammed the doors shut. Two guards ran over to Sherman's cell to make sure it was closed. One of the guards was Susan. She smiled at Sherman when she saw he was okay. She and the other guards moved on down the hall.

Sherman grabbed all four of his knives from under the bed and the one in his waistband and hid them along with the drugs under his lockers. He then went to the bars to watch the commotion that ensued on the tier. Some of the inmates refused to lie down, so they were beaten and handcuffed.

It took two hours before the bodies and the tier were cleaned up. Sherman was sitting on his bunk when six guards in armor and Major Brazil came to his cell door. Sherman looked up when the cell door came open.

"Lay down now!!" shouted Major Brazil.

Sherman thought they were coming just to do a cell check, but when Sherman laid down with his stomach on the floor, he was handcuffed and pulled to his feet.

"What the fuck y'all think y'all are doing!?" asked Sherman.

Major Brazil came and stood in front of Sherman, "Shut up, Ford!!"

Brazil nodded to the other guards.

"Take him out!" Brazil shouted.

The guards walked Sherman off the tier. He was escorted into a spacious luxuriously furnished office. The entire interior was a peach color. There was a long wooden desk in front of a window that stretched from ceiling to floor and spanned the length of the wall. The desk was stacked with files and papers. A gold name plate was at the end of the desk. The name on it was hard to see. Sherman took a seat in one of the chairs in front of the desk. He glanced back when he heard the door close. He saw a Black man in his mid forties. He was well dressed with a thick mustache. This man was the Warden Blackmon.

The Warden patted Major Brazil on his shoulder as he walked pass him. Then he stood in front of Sherman. He sized Sherman up before pointing at Sherman but staring at the Major.

"Is this him?" Warden Blackmon said, sarcastically.

The guards nodded their heads confirming Mr. Ford's identity.

"Okay then," said the Warden Blackmon. "How are you doing, Mr. Ford?"

Sherman was frowning up at the man.

"Who the fuck are you?" Sherman barked.

The Warden started smiling.

"I'm sorry, please forgive my bad manners. I am Warden Blackmon," he said, apologetically.

"Why in the hell did you call me up here!?" Sherman demanded.

"Mr. Ford, your name has been coming up in a lot of prison killings. This type of behavior is *not* and will *not* be tolerated in my prison! Do you understand?" Warden Blackmon stated.

"I don't know what you're talking about." Sherman said as he looked out the window.

The Warden shouted back at Sherman.

"Do not sit here and disrespect my intelligence, you piece of shit!!" Warden Blackmon said ferociously.

Sherman laughed hysterically. This infuriated the Warden. He grabbed and snatched Sherman out of his seat. He held him inches from his face. He stared straight in his eyes.

"Boy! I'll rip your motherfucking heart out!!" Warden Blackmon screamed.

Sherman became mad and looked insanely into the Warden's eyes.

"Get the fuck off me," Sherman calmly said.

The Warden released his firm grip on Sherman and pushed him back in his seat. Sherman continued staring angrily into the Warden's eyes.

"Mr. Ford, you have only been in my prison about six months and you have built up a threatening reputation. Inmates have dropped over two hundred notes on you stating that you ran up in Mr. Jackson's cell November seventeen and stabbed him to death. You killed James Barrow on December the second in the shower. You beat Mr. Howell Grave to death with a weight in the courtyard. You stabbed Mr. James Tyson to death while he was lifting weights. The weights fell on the man's neck but you continued to stab him even though he was already dead. You are a very dangerous and vicious animal. What do you have to say for yourself?" Warden Blackmon demanded.

"I don't know what you are talking about," said Sherman. "I have not done any of those things you just accused me of."

"Mr. Ford, I have not accused you of anything. Your fellow inmates sent me these letters. It seems the population is terrified of you. I have been told you are selling drugs in my prison. This is something else I will not tolerate." Warden Blackmon said, confidently.

"If you believe I have done these things," said Sherman, "then why haven't I been formally charged?"

"I do believe you have done these things but the inmates will not testify against you. I don't even know their names. I only received their notes. I just wanted to warn you. If I or any of my guards catch you in the wrong, you will be viciously punished," Warden Blackmon said, smiling.

Sherman smiled up at Warden, "I'm afraid."

Warden Blackmon started grinning, "Don't be afraid, Mr. Ford. Just watch your back."

"Warden, you are a dangerous man," Sherman said, grinning.

"No, I just get my way... by any means necessary," Warden Blackmon said, grinning.

"Is this all?" Sherman said, impatiently.

"Are you in a rush to go back to your little cage?" Warded Blackmon asked, sarcastically.

"No, just want to get the fuck out of your ugly ass face." Sherman replied.

The Warden leaned within inches of Sherman's nose.

"Do NOT let this ugly face be the last face you see in your dark cell." Warden Blackmon threatened.

Sherman smiled.

"Mr. Ford, you have a great sense of humor but I know a lot of men who died laughing." Warden Blackmon said as he stood, "Mr. Ford, if your name comes up in anything else, I mean anything else, I will have your ass shipped behind The Wall so fast, you will think it was a dream."

Sherman let out a deep breath.

"That ain't nothing but another prison."

The Warden started smiling.

"You know that is where the big boys play?" the Warden replied.

"I am a big boy!" Sherman calmly replied.

"A lot of men, whom you have hurt, have family members behind The Wall," Warden Blackmon warned

"I dance with death every day, so do you want to tango?" Sherman said.

"You're going to die in prison, Mr. Ford. Don't think you're going home because you will only disappoint yourself. You have managed to get yourself killed and you only had such a small amount of time with us. Stupid is what you are. You are a flunky, Mr. Ford. Only a flunky would do the things you have done. Five years. You could have made parole in a matter of months. I know your parole date was rescheduled, but you're supposed to go up real soon. Such a shame you won't be granted parole. It's like you were charged and convicted of those deaths. Blame it on stupidity," Warden Blackmon said, smirking

"Mr. Blackman, fuck you! Fuck those deaths and fuck your mama!" Sherman barked.

The Warden instantly punched Sherman in his mouth with his fist. Sherman's head jerked to the side. He gave the Warden the death stare then he spit some blood on the carpet and started smiling.

"I think you loosened my tooth." Sherman snickered.

The Warden leaned back over to Sherman.

Sherman got serious, "Don't hit me again!"

"Did that scare you!?" Warden Blackmon said, smiling

Then the Warden stood back up and waved his arm toward the door.

"Get him out here!!" he shouted.

As *the guards pulled Sherman out of the chair and walked him toward the door, he turned to look at the Warden.*

"Tell your momma I said, 'Hi!' " Sherman said, smiling.

"You just don't forget what I said!!" Warden Blackmon said as he pointed his finger at Sherman.

The guards walked Sherman into the hallway. As they walked down the hall, one of the guards started talking to Sherman.

"You should've just kept your mouth shut," said Major Brazil.

"Whatever!" Sherman shouted.

"Would you like to go to the medical unit to get that tooth looked at?" Major Brazil asked.

"No, my tooth isn't loose; I just wanted to make your boss feel good," Sherman said, sarcastically.

The guards walked Sherman down the tier. John was standing at his bars.

John asked, "What's up, Sherm? What happened? Where did they take you!?"

"We'll talk when we come out!" Sherman said.

"R-right." John replied.

When the guards locked Sherman in his cell, he stayed at his bars. He watched the guards do the same thing to John that they did to him. He walked away from the bars as the guards walked John down the tier. Sherman sat on his bunk and began reading.

Chapter Fourteen

Next Day

Sherman, Brace and John met up on the tier. They all shook hands.

Brace spoke first, "Man, that motherfucking warden had me dragged out my damn cell. Then the punk going to try and threaten me! The chump said, 'If your name comes up in something else, you're going behind The Wall!' "

Sherman and John both busted out into laughter. Brace looked at the two men with a weird expression.

"Man, I'm not joking!" said Brace.

They both looked at how serious Brace was and busted out into laughter again.

John spoke "Calm down fool. He did that same shit to us."

"Motherfuckers were thrown off tiers and the warden threatens us!" said Brace.

"That motherfucker punched me in the mouth!" said Sherman.

John and Brace stared at Sherman in disbelief.

Sherman spoke shaking his head, "Yea, that punk hit me. I'm going to get his ass though."

Brace was feeling his throat. He seemed to be in some pain. Neither, Sherman or John noticed Brace's painful expression.

"Sherman, don't try to go at Warden Blackmon. You cannot win," said John.

Brace held his hand under his chin, "He's right."

Sherman sucked his teeth then he changed the subject.

"How many people died last night?" asked Sherman.

"I think it was two of the Brotherhoods and three Mexicans," answered John.

"Fuck'em," said Brace. "Let them kill each other."

Brace paused for a few seconds then he spoke again.

"I'm getting ready to go and get that motherfucking money! That chump, Paul, think that I'm playing. The Aryan and Mexicans saved his ass yesterday but he better have that money today."

"Let's go," said Sherman.

The three men walked up the steps to the second floor. They walked down to Paul's cell. He was in his cell doing sit-ups with his back to the door. Brace stood in the doorway with his palms on the door frame. When Paul went down to begin another sit-up, he spotted Brace's shoes first, and then he looked up at Brace's face. Brace was smiling down at him.

195

"Do you have my money, Fool?"

Paul rushed to stand. He smiled back at Brace, but stood at a distance. Sherman and John were leaning on the bars from the outside of the cell. Both had their hand's sticking through the bars. John held a twelve inch knife in his left hand. Paul noticed the knife then he looked Brace in his smiling face.

"Do you have my money or not?" asked Brace.

"Brace, man you know I'm good for it. My peoples just haven't sent me the money yet. Haven't I paid you every other time?" Paul said, smiling.

"I am not complaining about every other time. I want my money this time. So do you have it?" Brace said.

"Nah, not y—" Paul said as he shook his head.

Brace cut the man's words off when he started yelling at him.

"Bitch!! I do not want to hear no excuses! I want to see dead presidents! And a lot of them!"

"I ba, I ba, I ba…" Paul was terrified.

Brace's facial expression became hard and evil looking.

" '*I ba, I ba,*' shit!"

Brace pulled out a shank that looked like a sword! The man's eyes opened wide with fear.

"God no." Paul pleaded with his palms raised.

"God can't help you now motherfucker!" Brace barked.

"Brace, please!" Paul continued to plead.

Brace scanned the room. He spotted the television and saw its cord plugged into the wall. He pointed to it. Paul looked over at the television and started feeling kind of relieved.

"Oh, you can have that. Fuck that TV. You can have the radio and the fan too!" Paul said, joyfully.

Brace stared the man in his eyes. "I want the cord."

"Oh, you can have that." Paul said.

Paul went and snatched the cord out of the wall and the television. He smiled as he tried to hand the cord to Brace. Brace looked up at the position of the vent above the mirror over the toilet. Paul looked up at the vent as well, and then fear consumed him again.

"Tie it up to the vent," said Brace.

"What?" Paul said in shock.

Brace's grip became tighter around the handle of the homemade knife and he started walking towards Paul. The man backed up until he fell on top of his bed. Brace raised his sword above his head. Paul looked like he wanted to just disappear. He was overcome with fear; he raised his hands in the air, hoping to block the knife.

Paul pleaded with urgency, "Okay! Okay, I'll do it!"

"Get up then, Bitch!" Brace barked.

Brace backed up four steps. He watched the man with caution as the man got off of the bed. The man looked at Brace with pleading eyes.

"Bitch, step up on the toilet." Brace demanded.

"Brace, Man what's going on here? My peoples are going to be sending me the money." Paul said.

Sherman screamed in from the doorway, *"Stop playing and kill that bitch!"*

Brace and Paul glanced over at Sherman then they looked at each other.

"Brace, please don't kill me. I have a lot to live for. I'm still young." Paul pleaded.

"Bitch, if you don't do what I said, you will die young!" Brace snapped.

"Yes sir." Paul said.

As Paul stepped up on the side of the toilet, he laid the cord on the bed. Brace continued to talk to him.

"Nigga, you don't have shit to live for. You were a damn junky on the street stealing from your peoples. Now you're in jail spending their money on drugs. You ain't shit but a hazard to your family! Bitch, get on top of the sink and tie the damn cord through the vent!" Brace ordered.

The man was shaking uncontrollably as he grabbed the cord off of the bed. He continued to tremble as he inserted one end of the cord into one of the many holes in the vent. He struggled to get the inserted end out of another hole in the vent. The vent was positioned in the center of the ceiling.

Paul looked like he was going to cry, "Brace, I'm scared of heights."

"Well, Bitch, I suggest that you don't look down!" Brace said.

"Please, Brace, man." Paul pleaded.

Brace swung the sword swift and hard ripping into Paul's arm. The man screamed out in pure agony. Blood started trickling out the gash. He was screaming at the top of his lungs. Brace leaped up on top of the toilet behind him, grabbed the back of his head and slammed his face to the wall. He held the knife under the man's throat with the tip of the blade breaking his flesh. Paul was crying uncontrollably as Brace placed his mouth near the man's ear.

Brace was so mad he spoke through his clinched teeth, "You are going to do what I say or you're going to be the first headless nigga. Do you hear me? Now do what I said."

"Yes Brace, I will do what you say, just please don't kill me." Paul pleaded.

Brace jumped backwards off of the toilet but stood near the man's body.

The man climbed on top of the sink and continued to struggle to get the tip of the cord out. He finally got the tip of the cord to exit one of the holes in the vent.

"Tie the cord tight." Brace coached.

"Brace, Man, please, man. Please don't kill me,"
Paul continued to plead.

"Tie the damn thing before I chop your nuts off!"
Brace barked.

The man tied the cord in a strong knot.

"Now tie the cord around your neck," Brace said.

The man looked at Brace like he was crazy.

Brace spoke in a calm voice, "Tie the damn cord
around your neck, now."

The man's body shook uncontrollably.
Brace stared up at him with deep hatred. He cocked
the sword backwards.

"You either going to tie that damn cord around your
neck this time or I'm going to cut your
motherfucking body in half."

This time Paul tied the cord around his neck.
He tried to plead for his life once more, but before he
could get a word out, Brace shoved his legs off of the
sink. The man's arms swung up into the air as his
feet kicked and searched frantically for something to
step on. Brace started kicking Paul's legs to prevent
him from regaining balance. The cord finally
tightened and snapped the man's neck. His body
dangled in the air while his feet shook as his last
breath of life was released. Brace stepped up on the
toilet and looked into the dead man's eyes. The dead
man had a smile as the blood trickled from the
corners of his mouth. Brace causally walked out of
the cell.

Brace proceeded on down the tier with his friends following close behind him. He and the others stopped in front of his cell. Sherman leaned his back up against the bars. John stood to Sherman's left and Brace stood to his right near the open doorway.

"They will not find him until the 3:00 PM count," Sherman said.

John looked at Brace who was just looking at the two of them.

"Yea," John asked, "what took you so long? You let the man scream and some more shit."

Before Brace could respond, he grabbed his chest with his left hand and the wall with his right hand. He coughed terribly then went unconscious. His upper body fell into his cell. Both men looked in disbelief at his legs because that was all that was sticking out of the cell.
"Man, what in the fuck is going on!?" asked Sherman.

Both men ran to their friend's aid. Sherman stepped inside of the cell and turned Brace's body over on his back. Brace was out cold. Sherman felt for a pulse then he looked up at John.

"He's still alive," Sherman said.

"R-right," said John. "Let's get him up."

Sherman extended his hand toward John.

"Nah!" said Sherman. "We can't move him."

"What!?" exclaimed John.

201

"We don't know what's wrong with him."

Sherman noticed the lump in Brace's shirt. He lifted Brace's shirt to his chest. The lump was caused by the shank Brace had in his waistband. The shank had cut through Brace's flesh when he fell to the floor. The cut was about two inches deep. Sherman pulled the knife from Brace's waistband and laid it on the floor beside his foot. Sherman looked his friend in his face.

"Brace! Brace, can you hear me? Brace!" Sherman said with concern.

"We just can't leave him here," said John.

Sherman looked up at John and spoke, "Look, take this knife and my knife and put them under my bed, then go get the guards."

Sherman pulled his knife from his waistband and grabbed Brace's knife off the floor. He handed both of the weapons to John. John grabbed both of the weapons and lifted his shirt. John stuck both of the weapons in his waistband and pulled his shirt down over the weapons and disappeared from the doorway. Sherman turned back toward Brace.

"Brace! Brace can you hear me? John go get the medic," said Sherman.

Brace didn't respond.

"Brace?" Sherman asked, "What in the hell's wrong with you?"

Sherman looked back down at Brace's flesh wound. The cut was bleeding. Sherman stood up

*and walked over to Brace's sink. There was a stack
of four washcloths on the shelf beside the mirror. He
grabbed the first washcloth and then turned on the
faucet and wet the cloth. He turned the water off and
knelt back down beside his friend. He wiped Brace's
face with the cloth. Brace was still unconscious.
Sherman started wiping the blood from the cut only
to see more blood appear.*

"Damn John, what's taking you so long?" Sherman
mumbled.

*Sherman went back to the sink and ran more
water onto the cloth after he rinsed most of the blood
off of the cloth. He then went straight back over to
Brace's body and continued to try and wipe away the
blood. John, Corporal James, and Corporal Kritz
appeared in the doorway. Corporal James stepped
over Brace's lower body into the cell.*

"Would you please move back, Sir?" Corporal James
asked.

*Sherman stood up and backed away towards
Brace's bed. Corporal James knelt down beside
Brace's head.*

"Sir, can you hear me?" Corporal James said as he
tapped Brace on his shoulder.

"Man!" said Sherman, "I already did that! He needs
medical attention!"

*Corporal James looked back at Sherman
with an evil stare then he looked at Corporal Kritz
who was standing beside John in the doorway.*

"Call medical and tell them to get down here immediately," said Corporal James. "We have a man unconscious with a knife wound."

Corporal Kritz nodded his head and pulled out his walkie-talkie and called the medical unit. Corporal James pulled Brace's shirt up to his armpits. He spotted the wound from the knife. It looked to be as long as seven inches.

"Where is the knife?" asked Corporal James.

Sherman was frowning down at the guard like he didn't hear the question.

"What?" Sherman asked.

"Where is the knife?" Corporal James demanded.

"Knife? I don't know nothing about no damn knife." Sherman replied

Corporal James pointed at the wound on Brace's belly.

"This man was carrying a knife. He must have fallen on top of the knife when he passed out because this doesn't look like a stab wound. The wound looks to be maybe from his thigh on up to his chest, so where's the knife?" Corporal James replied in a calm but threatening tone.

"Man, I don't know nothing about no damn knife!" Sherman snapped.

"Were you with him when he went unconscious?" asked Corporal Kritz.

"No." Sherman replied.

Then Corporal James looked at John.

"Were you with him?"

John shook his head side to side, "No."

He didn't believe them and it showed. Then Rebecca and Nurse Rose walked into the cell. Corporal James backed away from Brace and stood beside Sherman. The two nurses knelt beside the unconscious man. She checked his pulse.

"He's still alive," she said with relief.

Nurse Rose looked up at Sherman, "Does he have any type of illnesses?"

Sherman hunched his shoulders, "Not that I know of."

Rebecca scanned the cut again.

"Where is the knife that he was carrying?" she questioned.

Corporal focused his attention on Sherman as he spoke to her, "I'm trying to find that out now."

Neither John nor Sherman responded. She looked at the doorway and saw that the two male nurses, Tom and Lou, had arrived with the stretcher.

"Tom and Lou! Come and get him so we can get him down to the medical Unit." she ordered.

John and Corporal Kritz moved from the doorway. Tom and Lou pulled the stretcher into the cell. Rebecca assisted them in lifting Brace's body onto the stretcher. The nurses left with the patient. Corporal James told Corporal Kritz to bring John into the cell. The guard did as he was told. Corporal James searched both men then he dismissed them. The guards left the cell right behind Sherman and John. The guards vacated the cell immediately after Sherman and John. They slammed the cell door shut and preceded down the tier. Sherman and John walked down to Sherman's cell.

Chapter Fifteen

EVENING

     *Sherman walked out of his cell. John and
another man leaned against Sherman's cell bars
when the man saw Sherman. The man raised up off
the bars and faced Sherman. Sherman walked over
to him and handed him a pebble of crack cocaine.
The man handed Sherman a twenty-dollar bill. He
took the money and stuffed it into his jeans pants
pocket. The man smiled at him and walked away.
Sherman walked over to John. John was picking his
teeth with a plastic spoon. When Sherman stood in
front of John, he looked at Sherman and stuffed the
spoon into his shirt pocket.*

"What's up?" asked John. "What do you want to do?"

     Sherman hunched his shoulders.

"Nothing fo'real. I want to find out what's up with
Brace." Sherman replied.

"You haven't seen your girl yet?" John asked.

"Nah, she doesn't work until tonight. She should be
getting on duty now." Sherman said.

     *Sherman took his hand and ran it against
his face. He looked at his watch.*

"Why did they let us out so late?" Sherman asked.

"What, did you forget the lynching today?" John said, smiling.

Sherman had his left hand on his forehead.

"Damn, that's right. As a matter of fact, I did forget about it. Who did the administration question?"

John hunched his shoulders.

"I don't know. They didn't come fucking with us, so fuck it." John replied.

"I hope they don't come fucking with us." Sherman said, shaking his head with a look of annoyance.

"The Warden believes he scared the shit out of us with his bullshit threat. I don't think he'll think it was us." John said, smiling.

Sherman grinned.

"If I hear ya' name again, ya'll are going behind the wall!' " imitated Sherman.

Both John and Sherman burst into laughter.

"Could you believe that bitch? Ha! Ha! Damn, I needed that laugh." John said, laughing.

Sherman grinned.

"Oh, yea, I finished off that shit I had," said John.

"I only have three more twenty pieces to go but we have more than enough to get two ounces. I'm going to tell Susan that I need her to pick it up for us again. She might still be mad at me about that baby shit though. So we might be shit out of luck," said Sherman.

"That bitch better not do us like that," said John.
"I'm sure I can get her to do it." Sherman bragged.

Outlaw and Acid, two Aryan Brothers with tattoos covering their entire arms walked over to John and Sherman. John leaned back on the bars with his right foot on the bars. Sherman turned around to face the two men. Acid smiled at Sherman and John. Neither Sherman nor John smiled back. Outlaw stood there expressionless with his arms folded across his chest.

"What's up?" asked Sherman, daringly.

"Yo, Bro, do you have any of those twenty pieces. I want to buy five of them, "Acid replied, cheerfully.

Sherman looked the man straight in his eyes.

"I only have three left."

Acid *smiled and nodded his head.*

"Yea, I can buy those? I got money right here," said Acid.

Acid reached into his pocket and pulled out five wrinkled twenty dollar bills .

"R-right, stay right here." Sherman said.

Sherman walked into his cell. Acid started talking to John. Outlaw continued to stand there with his arms folded across his chest.

"Bro, I heard something happened to Brace. Is he all right?" Acid asked with what seemed to be genuine concern.

John was looking at both men. He had started picking his teeth with the spoon again.

"Yea, he's alright." Brace replied.

"Bro, what happened to him?" asked Acid.

John stuck the spoon into his shirt pocket.

"You're asking too many questions." John replied.

Acid nodded his head in agreement as he continued to smile.

"I understand," said Acid, "My fault, Bro."

Sherman came back out of his cell and walked over to the two white men. He handed Acid the pebbles and at the same time, stared Outlaw in his eyes. Neither man blinked until Acid handed Sherman the money. Sherman looked at the money then stuffed it into his pocket. The Aryan Brothers walked off. Sherman walked over and leaned against the bars beside John.

"Well, now I am finished," said Sherman. "One thing about them white boys, when they do come to purchase, they come to spend some money."

John nodded his head in agreement but never looking at Sherman.

"Yup. I don't know what's up with that other cracker?" John said with suspicion.

"Fuck him." Sherman said, smiling.

Philly, *a big muscle bound brown skinned man walked over to John and Sherman. Sherman and John both shook the man's hand. Philly smiled at them.*

"What's up, fellas'!?" Philly said with excitement.

"Aint shit," said John, happily.

"Nothing much. What's up with you?" asked Sherman.

"Not too much. Do you have any dime pieces of caine?" Philly asked in almost a whisper.

John and Sherman shook their heads no.

"Nah, we just sold our last to the white boys." John confided.

Philly looked disappointed, but managed to make a smile.

"Damn... Okay," Philly replied.

The man rubbed his chin and then he smiled and looked at Sherman.

"Sherman, what do you think about the game?" Philly asked.

Sherman looked puzzled.

"What game?"

"The Redskins and Philly game tonight!" Philly said with a look of surprise.

Sherman started smiling.

"Skins are going to beat that ass!" Sherman said with excitement.

Philly started holding his stomach laughing.

"Sheeed!" Philly replied.

"Watch. They're playing here in Washington, too!" Sherman shouts back, humorously.

"You trying to bet then?" Philly said with less humor.

"Bet what?" Sherman said with interest.

"Twenty packs of cigarettes!" Philly said, smiling.

Sherman looked the man seriously in his eyes.

"You're not trying to do that." Sherman warned.

Philly still smiled.

"Sheeed! That's easy money there!" Philly yelp.

"Do you have the money?" Sherman seriously asked.

"Of course." Philly replied with a look of shock.

"So when do we pay up?" Sherman replied.

"Tonight after the game." Philly said.

"Man, do you have the cigarettes?" Sherman said in almost a threatening tone.

Philly still smiled.

"Hell yea. So are you betting or what?" Philly replied.

Sherman never cracked a smile.

"Yea, I'll bet you. Look, I play a lot of games but I don't play about my money. So if you lose, have mine." Sherman warned.

"You better have mine 'cause Philly got this in the bag," Philly responded with confidence.

He extended his hand to Sherman and they shook hands.

"Then we have a bet," said Sherman.

"You damn right!" said Philly.

"Have my money when you lose." Sherman said.

"Ain't no calling the bet off at the last minute," Philly joked.

"Just have my money. I will have your money if I lose." Sherman said.

Philly turned and walked back down the tier. Sherman looked over at John who was shaking his head.

"What are you shaking your head for?" asked Sherman.

John looked over at his friend.

"If you wanted to kill him, you should've did it right here." John said.

"What!?" asked Sherman.

"That man doesn't have no money. Didn't you hear him ask for a dime piece? If he had twenty packs of cigarettes, he would of asked to buy a twenty piece of cocaine," John informed him.

Sherman just looked across the tier.

"He better have my money," said Sherman, threateningly.

"Watch, he doesn't have the money," said John.

"Then he will be leaving in the Dewitt truck," Sherman said, reassuringly.

John looked down the tier and saw Susan walking up to them. John then looked at Sherman.

"Here comes your baby mother," John said with a smirk.

Sherman looked down the tier and saw Susan coming. He looked at John's smiling face.

"That's not my damn baby mother!" he said.

John busted into laughter then he walked down the tier in the direction of Susan. They spoke but John continued to walk. Susan walked over to Sherman, who still leaned up against the wall.

"What's up?" asked Susan.

Sherman acted like he had an attitude by not looking at her.

"Nothing." Sherman replied.

Susan stuck both her hands in her pockets.

"What's wrong with you?" she said, hesitantly.

Sherman glanced over at her and then looked back across the tier.

"Nothing." Sherman replied.

"Why are you mad?" she looked at him innocently.

"I'm not mad." Sherman replied.

"Well, look at me then," she pleaded.

Sherman turned and faced Susan still leaning up against the wall.

"What's up?" Sherman said, nonchalantly.

Sherman took his left palm and rubbed his eye.

"I came to tell you," said Susan, "your friend Brace is all right. He will be leaving the medical unit today."

"Okay."

Susan looked mad. She didn't like him not talking to her.

"Why in the hell are you ignoring me!?" she shouted.

"I am not ignoring you." he said lowering his voice and scanning the area.

Susan spoke in an angry tone of voice, but not loud.

"I bet this will bring a smile to your face. I'm not pregnant." she snapped.

Susan turned around and started walking away. She stopped walking when Sherman called her.

"Susan!" Sherman barked.

She turned around and looked at him.

"What!" she said, irritably.

Sherman looked mad.

"Come here, now!" he replied.

Susan smiled and walked back over to him. When she stood in front of him, she had her right hand on her hip. Sherman looked angry.

"What's your motherfucking problem walking away from me?" he demanded.

Susan's smile disappeared. She was now staring at Sherman expressionless.

"What is wrong with you?" she begged.

Sherman wasn't smiling.

"What the fuck is wrong with you?" he shot back.

"What did I do? You are the one acting like you have a problem." she said, whining.

"You walked up to me and talking this bullshit about, I should be happy you aren't pregnant. What you think that's some type of game?" he asked.

Susan looked confused.

"Hold up, I only said that because you were acting crazy. I thought you didn't want no baby by a white girl anyway," she shot back angrily but needing an answer.

"I was fucking you, wasn't I?" he said with a lighter tone.

Susan rolled her eyes at Sherman.

"Yea, you were fucking me. Apparently, that was all it meant to you." she responded.

Sherman looked up at the wall above his head.

"Yea, whatever!" he said.

When Sherman looked back at Susan, she had her lips poked out, face frowning and her right hand on her hip.

"What do you mean, whatever?" she demanded.

"Look Susan, I don't want to be beefin' with you. I apologize for whatever I may have said to make you mad."

Then he smiled.

"So can we be lovers again?" He said in a whisper as he lowered his chin and smiled at her with his eyes.

Susan looked at him in disbelief then she rolled her eyes and smiled.

"You are a trip. Your dick must have just got hard," she replied, shaking her head.

Sherman still smiled.

"It did. So are we going to take care of that problem," Sherman asked.

Susan was still smiling, "Whatever."

"So what's up?" he replied.

"We will see." she said, fighting to hold back her smile.

"Oh, yea," said Sherman, "I need you to pick up some more shit for me."

"Are you going to make me lose my job?" asked Susan with a frown.

"We don't want that to happen... Look, call me to the medical unit tonight. I'll bring the money to you, and then I want some," he said.

"Only way you ever doing it to me again is if you make love to me," she warned.

"I don't eat no pussy," said Sherman.

"I don't want you to eat my pussy. I just don't want what we do to only mean a fuck to you," she admitted.

"Okay, I'll make passionate love to you then," he said, humorously.

Susan grinned.

"Meaning you are going to eat some pussy then," she jokingly replied.

"Sheeed!" he replied with disgust.

Susan grinned.

"I have to go, Sherman, I will call you up," she warned.

"Okay," he replied.

Susan turned around and walked down the tier. Sherman saw Brace and John walking toward the steps. Brace was moving extremely slow. John stood behind him, preparing to assist him if needed, as Brace climbed two steps. Sherman ran down to them. Sherman smiled up at Brace.

"What's up, Sherm?" asked Brace with exhaustion.

"Nothing much. Are you alright?" Sherman asked with true concern.

"Yea. Well, I will know in a couple of weeks," Brace said with a sign of worry.

Sherman looked puzzled.

"I don't understand," Sherman replied.

"I let the doctors talk me into taking an AIDS test. The test will be back in a few weeks," Brace replied.

"You'll be alright no matter what," Sherman said, reassuringly.

"That shit is easy to say. Whatever you do, don't fuck with the faggies," Brace said as he wiped slobber from his mouth.

"You don't have to ever worry about that! I have Susan for right now and when she's gone, no problem, I love jerking off," Sherman said, humorously.

The three men smiled. Brace tapped his hand on the railing.

"Well fellas, I'm tired, so I'm going in here to rest up. Hopefully, I won't miss the game. I will holla at ya'll later," Brace replied.

"Sherman, let me make sure he gets in and I'mma come right back," said John.

"R-right. I'll lay right here for you," said Sherman.

"Man, I don't need you watching my back. I've been a gangster all my life," Brace mumbled as he made his way up the steps.

Brace walked into his cell. Then John met up with Sherman. They headed toward their cells.

"Is your girl going to take care of that?" asked John.

"Yea," answered Sherman, "I have to go call Ella, so she can call my main man."

"Cool. Are you going to watch the game?"

"Yea, after I make the call."

They stopped at John's cell. He looked at his watch.

"The game is getting ready to come on now," said John.

John pulled a big roll of money out of his pocket and handed it to Sherman. They are not supposed to have money in prison but inmates smuggle it in when they are on a family visit or have a crooked guard bring it in.

"That's eighteen hundred," said John.

"Cool," said Sherman. "I'll holla at you after the game."

"R-right."

John walked into his cell and Sherman walked down to the dayroom and called Ella. After he finished talking to Ella, he went into his cell to watch the football game.

Chapter Sixteen

As Sherman, Brace, John and about three hundred other inmates left the prison cafeteria; John looked up at the gray clouds. The cement on the walkway was wet from the earlier drizzle.

"It's going to rain again soon," predicted John.

Brace seemed more like himself. He was walking upright and talking clearly. He looked up at the gray clouds.

"Sure is," agreed Brace.

The three men walked into the middle of the crowd. Brace glanced down at his wristwatch then he looked at Sherman.

"Sherm, did you watch the game?"

Sherman started smiling as he reminisced about the football game.

"Yea, I saw it." Sherman laughed.

"Them damn Skins got their man today! I lost six packs because those motherfuckers won!" Brace said with excitement.

Sherman looked at Brace with a grin.

"Never go against the grain! Never count the Skins out. The Skins just put twenty packs in my pocket.

Yea! I pick mine up after I get up out of the shower!" Sherman exclaimed.

John wasn't smiling when he spoke, "Man, that junkie don't have no damn twenty packs of cigarettes."

"We will see," said Sherman.

Sherman grabbed hold of the entrance door and the men walked inside the building. They headed down the tier toward John's and Sherman's cell.

"Man, that junkie better have my money," said Sherman with a sneer.

John was shaking his head, "I told you up front, Sherman."

"All I have to say is, he better get mines," Sherman said without any emotions.

Brace held his left hand over his mouth as he yawned.

"Well, I am getting tired. What are ya' going to do?" Brace asked.

"I'm getting ready to get into the shower," said Sherman.

"I'm going into the dayroom to play poker or something," said John.

"I'm with that!" said Brace.

"Well," said Sherman, "let me run and get my shower gear, and then we can roll."

Sherman walked into his cell and gathered the things he needed to take a shower. He walked out of his cell wearing Timberland boots, blue jean shorts, a tank top t-shirt, and carrying a shower bag. He looked over at his two friends who were still talking. John had his back up against Sherman's cell bars. Brace stood in front of John.

"Ya' ready?" asked Sherman.

Both men looked at Sherman.

"Yea, let's roll," said John.

John lifted up off the bars and the three men headed down the tier.

"Sherman, when is your white girl going to pick up the crack?" asked Brace.

"I talked to my *baby mother* before I watched the game. She's going to get that tonight. Susan supposed to be calling me to the medical unit tonight. So, I'll tell her to go pick that up from Ella," Sherman said.

"Sherman, you be wearing that white pussy out! Damn! I would love to hit that," said Brace.

"I'll tell her you're trying to go. I doubt it if she goes for it. Didn't you already ask me that though?" Sherman asked.

Brace hunched his shoulders.

"Probably, I'm just playing, though. Well, maybe I am not playing but I don't want you to cut your own throat," Brace said, jokingly.

"Man, it ain't nothing but some pussy. Either she is going to fuck you or she's not," Sherman boasted.

"Sherman, that's okay, I don't want you to ask her," Brace replied.

"Alright then," Sherman said.

John pulled the dayroom door open and the three men walked into the crowded room. A lot of prisoners looked back toward the door to see who was coming in. Some of the men spoke to the three men. John and Brace walked over to one of the tables. There were four men at the table playing cards. Sherman spoke to a few of the men and headed toward the back room. While Sherman was walking, he caught a ping-pong ball that went astray from the ping-pong table. He handed the ball to one of the ping-pong players. He walked into the back where the showers were. He placed his shower bag on the wall beside the showers then he took off his shorts, boxer shorts and t-shirt. He walked into the showers with his boots on carrying his soap, shampoo and washcloth. There were six other men taking showers. Sherman spotted Philly, the he made the football bet with. Philly was standing under the shower head. The water was splashing on his back as he washed his chest. He was staring at Sherman as Sherman walked over to him. Sherman wasn't mad. He was smiling. He stopped walking and stood in front of the man.

Sherman was still smiling, "Yea! I told you! So can I get paid?" Sherman said.

Philly was looking evilly at Sherman, "Don't you see me taking a motherfucking shower!!"

Sherman's smile turned into a smirk, "What!!? Man, where in the fuck is my money!?"

The other men in the shower were looking at the two men argue. One of the other men in the same shower exited. Philly was still gritting on Sherman.

"What do you mean, where's your money? Nigga, I won the bet!" Philly barked.

"Bitch! You better get my money! Nigga, don't be trying to play mind games with me," Sherman barked back.

"Sherman, yo, you better get the fuck out of my face!" Philly threaten as he put his bar of soap down.

Sherman looked at the man in disbelief "What!!?"

Sherman nodded his head.

"R-right," Sherman replied.

Sherman backed up and turned around. He walked back over to the wall, where he put his shower bag. Sherman didn't see Philly creep past him. Sherman pulled his knife from his shower bag and placed the shower bag on top of the wall. He walked back into the shower with his knife gripped in his right hand. There were only two men in the shower now. Sherman looked toward the shower where his enemy was. The shower was empty. He looked over at one of the men who was still in the shower. The man was looking Sherman straight in his eyes.

"Where did that dude go?" Sherman asked pointing to the shower Philly had occupied.

The man hunched his shoulders and continued to wash up. Sherman then turned around and walked into the dayroom holding his knife in his hand. All of the men in the dayroom stopped what they were doing and looked at Sherman. John and Brace stood up from the table they were sitting at and walked over to Sherman. All of the other men in the room kept their eyes on the three men.

"What's up, man?" asked John.

"Man, I'm going to kill that nigga!" said Sherman.

"Who!? What happened?" asked Brace.

"That bitch ass nigga I made that bet with! That nigga tried to run game on me! Man, I'm going to kill that bitch," Sherman said.

John glanced around the room then he looked back at Sherman.

"Well, he ain't in here," said John. "So, won't you go get dressed?"

"I will get him. Look man, I'm getting back into the shower," said Sherman.

"R-right," said Brace, "we'll be out here."

The three men looked toward the table where two men were arguing, "Man, you are cheating!! One of the men said, "Fuck You! You know I don't have to cheat you" the other man said. Then a third man at the table spoke, "Man, ya fools playing or what!??" Both of the men nodded their heads up and down and said "Yeah!" They continued playing cards. John and Brace looked back at Sherman.

227

"I'm gone back into the shower," said Sherman.

Sherman turned around and walked into the back room. He got back into the shower and started washing up. He poured shampoo into his hair and started washing it. While he was washing the back of his head, he was hit with a lock in a sock on the top of his hand. Sherman fell into the wall face first, holding the back of his head. Philly cracked Sherman across the side of his head again. Sherman was in too much pain to swing back at Philly. He held up his hand to try and block the blows.

Philly was yelling, "Bitch Motherfucker!!"

He cracked Sherman across his hands. Sherman made a dash for the exit. Philly cracked him again across his back with the lock and sock. He stumbled but he didn't fall. He kept running and ran into the dayroom. Philly was running behind him. Everyone in the dayroom quickly turned their heads when they heard   Sherman storm through the backdoors.

Philly cracked Sherman across the shoulder with the lock and sock. Sherman stumbled and fell on top of one of the men playing ping-pong. Both men fell on top of the ping-pong table. Philly continued to hit Sherman across his body. When Brace and John noticed Sherman being attacked, both men jumped up and snatched their knives from their waist.

Philly saw both John and Brace as they ran over toward him. He hit Sherman one more time across his arm and ran out of the dayroom doors. Brace started to chase him but he quickly became out of breath so he stopped.

*John ran over to Sherman, who was still
lying on top of the other man holding his head.
Brace was soon at John's side. They pulled Sherman
off of the man. Sherman screamed out in agony.
Brace grabbed John's knife from John's hand as he
held Sherman. Brace stuck both weapons in his waist.
Sherman's head was busted and he had bruises on his
upper body. He was very dizzy.*

"Man, you have to go to the medical unit," said John.

Sherman spoke in pain, "Man, I'm alright."

"Sheeed!" said John.

"Man, I'm going to kill that nigga. Man, let me go,
John." Sherman muttered, drowsily.

"Nah man, come on!" John said.

*John was trying to walk Sherman to the back
where the showers were. But Sherman couldn't walk.
He was still in immense pain. His legs were wobbly
and he was holding his head, which bled profusely.*

"Man, let me go!" said Sherman.

"R-right," said John.

*John released Sherman and he tried to take
a step. His knees buckled and he fell against the wall.
John and Brace pulled him off the wall.*

"Man, you are going to the medical unit," said John.
"Brace, go get his clothes."

*Brace disappeared through the back doors.
He came back through the doors with Sherman's
clothes and bag in his hand. John held Sherman up*

while Brace pulled his pants up over his boots and up to his waist.

"Come on," said John. "Brace help me with him."

All of the other men in the dayroom just watched the three men. One of the other men in the dayroom opened the door for them to exit. Sherman's friends walked him onto the tier. He looked down at the Bubble at the other end of the tier.

As they walked down the tier, Sherman started talking. He held his towel over his head wound.

"Man, don't neither one of ya touch him. He's mine," Sherman demanded.

John and Brace looked at each other.

"Man, I'm serious," said Sherman. "I owe that fool."

John nodded his head in agreement.

"R-right. I won't go at him," John replied.

Sherman looked at Brace.

"I'm serious, Brace."

"R-right. I won't touch him unless he comes after me," Brace warned.

Sherman stopped by John's cell. John and Brace looked at him. John still held Sherman up by his shoulders.

"Come on, Sherman," said John.

"Man, help me put my shirt on," said Sherman.

John and Brace looked at Sherman in wonder. Sherman still spoke as if he was in pain.

"Man, I have to put my shirt on. I'm going to tell the guards I slipped in the shower."

"R-right," said John, "Lift both your arms up."

Sherman tried to lift his left hand above his head, but his ribs hurt too badly. He moaned in pain and dropped both of his arms to his side.

"Man, my damn ribs are killing me," Sherman said. "I'm going to kill that bitch."

John looked at Brace.

"Brace, hold him up," said John. "I'm going into my cell and get him a jacket to put on."

Brace then grabbed hold of Sherman's shoulders. John disappeared into his cell. Sherman started shivering. Brace laughed at him.

As Sherman's teeth chattered, he looked at Brace, "Man, I'm cold as a motherfucker."

John came out of his cell holding a dark blue jean jacket. While Brace held Sherman up, John slipped the jacket up his arms. Sherman looked at his two friends.

"Man, these motherfuckers are going to try and put me on bed rest," Sherman said with regret.

Sherman placed the white blood stained towel back to his head wound.

231

"Come on," said Brace.

The three men continued their walk down to The Bubble. The other inmates watched them with curiosity and whispers. Once they were in front of The Bubble, John knocked on the door. Corporal James, Corporal Kritz and two other guards were in The Bubble. Corporal James walked over to the door. He stared at the three inmates curiously.

Then he spotted the bloodstains on the towel that Sherman held to his head. He waved his hand signaling the three men to step away from the door. Brace frowned at the guard because he believed the guard was telling them to get away from The Bubble. When he noticed that Brace had misinterpreted his signal, he turned his head sideways and spoke to the other guards in The Bubble. Corporal Kritz walked to the intercom and pushed a button.

"Hey guys, step away from the door so the officer can exit the booth." Corporal Kritz ordered.

Sherman and the others took four steps away from the door. Corporal James opened the door and stepped onto the tier. He walked over to Sherman and stopped. He pointed to Sherman's head. Sherman was still holding the towel over the wound. Corporal Kritz was standing at the closed door watching them.

"What happened?" asked Corporal James.

Sherman looked at him evilly.

"I fell on that damn slippery ass shower floor!" Sherman barked.

Corporal James pulled out his walkie-talkie and called the medical unit. Then he placed the walkie-talkie back in its case on his belt.

Corporal James spoke with concern, "Are you in any pain?"

Sherman grimaced as he said, "You damn right I am!"

"The medic should be here in a few seconds. You can't stand up on your own?" Corporal James inquired.

John answered for Sherman, "He tried it once and his knees buckled so we decided to help him stand."

The guard nodded his head in agreement.

"I would have done the same," Corporal James replied.

Corporal James looked toward the bars at the entrance of the tier. Nurse Rebecca, Nurse Tom, Nurse Lou, and Officer Jim came through the open bars pulling a stretcher. Corporal James looked back at Sherman.

"Here they are now," Corporal James replied.

The medical people came over to Sherman. Rebecca directed him to sit on top of the stretcher. Brace and one of the male nurses helped him up onto the top of the stretcher.

"Go ahead and lay back," Rebecca said.

Sherman lay back on the stretcher. Inmates stood all around, about five feet away from Sherman and the others. They just looked at what was going on. Corporal Kritz and another officer exited The Bubble. The officers asked the onlookers to move back, which they did. Some of the inmates made smart remarks. The nurses strapped Sherman down on the stretcher. He looked over at John and Brace and smiled.

"I guess I will see ya'll later."

Then the nurses rolled Sherman through the open metal gate.

Chapter Seventeen

Susan had just let three inmates into the medical unit waiting room, when the nurses rolled Sherman in on the stretcher. Officer Jim trailed behind the nurses. Once Susan locked the inmates in the holding pen, she looked over to the medic. She saw Sherman laying on the stretcher looking at her. She almost yelled his name in worry but she caught herself. She held her hand over her mouth and her eyes began to water. After seeing all the blood on his head, she knew he was hurt. The medics rolled him into a room and closed the door.

Officer Jim went and sat in his chair near the medic unit entrance door. He leaned his head back onto the white walls and closed his eyes. Susan walked over to him. When Officer Jim sensed someone was standing in front of him, he opened his eyes and saw Susan. "She looks worried," Officer Jim thought to himself.

"Jim," said Susan, "what happened to that man y'all just brought in here?"

Officer Jim placed both of his hands on his legs.

"He said he fell in the showers. Personally, I think he is lying," Officer Jim replied.

"Why do you say that?" she asked.

"He has a lot of scars on his head, back, face and neck. That man would have had to have fallen a lot of times to have all of those bruises," Officer Jim replied.

"Is he hurt bad though? I mean is he alright?" she asked.

Officer Jim looked at Susan suspiciously. She noticed the change in Jim's facial expression.

"Why are you so concerned?" asked Officer Jim.

Susan smiled and hunched her shoulders.

"Because I saw all of that blood and if he dies, we have a lot of paperwork to do.... I mean you do," she said, forcing herself to laugh.

Officer Jim smiled up at Susan.

Nurse Lou and Nurse Tom removed the straps from around Sherman's upper-body as Rebecca continued examining the bruises on his head. Sherman started watching Nurse Rose look through a cabinet on the wall. The cabinet was full of different kinds of medicine. Then he looked at Nurse Lou as he looked through a file cabinet for Sherman's medical file, while Nurse Tom looked through some papers on the desk by the door.

Rebecca was still looking at Sherman's head wounds. Nurse Rose positioned medical items to treat his wounds on a gray tray and pushed the tray near Rebecca.

Rebecca stepped in front of Sherman and signaled him to look straight up at the ceiling, which he did. She shined the small flashlight into both of his eyes. She then opened Sherman's jacket to examine his chest. She could not believe all of the bruises she saw.

Sherman noticed the look on her face as she examined him. She took both of her hands and pressed them down on a bruise on his ribs. Sherman bit his lip to stop from screaming. She looked quizzically at his face and then she pressed her hands down on a bruise again. He bit down on his lip again.

"Mr. Ford, what really happened to you?" Rebecca asked while looking him seriously in his eyes.

"I fell in the showers," Sherman said.

Sherman ran his left hand across his forehead.

"Mr. Ford, I don't know how to treat you if I don't know what really happened to you," she warned.

"I fell coming out of the showers," he replied.

Rebecca looked down at Sherman's soaked boots then back at him.

"Mr. Ford, I don't have to be a detective to know you wore your boots into the shower. You have multiple wounds and bruises on your chest, as well as your head, back and face. Apparently one fall couldn't have caused all of this. In fact, many falls couldn't have caused all of these wounds. So, you had to have been beaten with a heavy object. So, Mr. Ford, I'm going to have to run some x-rays on you. You may have some broken bones," Rebecca said.

She placed her hand on Sherman's left shoulder and looked him seriously in his eyes.

"Mr. Ford, if somebody is trying to kill you? Please allow me to help you."

Sherman became angry. His teeth were together tightly as he spoke. He had a sinister look on his face.

"Bitch! You better do what you have to do and let me get the fuck out of here. If you ask me another goddamn question, I will beat your ass in here," he said.

Rebecca saw how serious Sherman was and became frightened by his threats. She knew what the inmates were capable of. She stood and put her hands into her white jacket pockets and smiled at him. Then she walked over to Nurse Tom. He was still looking through the papers on the desk.

"Would you please start taking X-rays of Mr. Ford? I have to step out for a minute," Rebecca commanded.

Nurse Tom nodded his head in agreement.

"Yes, I'll start the X-rays," Nurse Tom replied.

Rebecca nodded her head as Nurse Tom walked over to Sherman. Then Rebecca left the room, closing the door behind her. She walked over to Susan and Officer Jim.

Officer Jim still sat in the chair. Susan was standing near him. They turned their attention to Rebecca. Rebecca smiled at them as she stood there with both of her hands in her pockets.

"Good evening officers," Rebecca said.

Officer Jim stood up. He looked concerned.

"Is there a problem, Doc?" asked Officer Jim.

"Yes," Rebecca replied, sternly.

"Stay here," said Officer Jim to her.

When Jim started to walk, Rebecca grabbed his arm gently. Officer Jim looked at her and then she released his arm.

"It is not a problem like that, even though the patient has threatened me," Rebecca said with little concern.

"Excuse me!" said Susan.

Susan looked at her in disbelief. Rebecca looked over at her.

"Yes," Rebecca responded.

"What did you just say?" asked Susan.

"Mr. Ford told me he would beat my ass if I asked him any more questions," Rebecca replied.

Susan couldn't believe her ears.

"I will deal with him!" said Officer Jim, angrily.
Susan looked over to him.

"Jim, be cool," Susan said.

Officer Jim turned and looked at Susan.

"Didn't you hear Doc say he threatened her," said Officer Jim.

"Yes, I did... Doc what kinds of questions were you asking the inmate?" Susan asked.

" I came out here to talk with you two. I believe Mr. Ford's life may be in danger," she suggested.

"Huh?!" exclaimed Susan.

"Yes, I believe Mr. Ford was beaten with a heavy object. My assistants are taking X-rays of Mr. Ford now. I believe it is possible that he may have a few broken bones. The x-rays shall determine my theory. Mr. Ford continues to say he fell in the showers, which I find very hard to believe. He would have to have fallen numerous times landing on rocks to cause the kind of damage he has. I know these inmates will not tell anything that happened to them or anybody else but I thought I should inform you on my beliefs," Rebecca said.

Susan looked at Officer Jim. His facial expression said, "I told you." Then Susan looked at the doctor.

"I hope you will have this matter investigated," said Rebecca.

"Yes," said Susan, "we will. So is that why the inmate became angry with you?"

"Yes, Ma'am. I would feel much safer if one of you would accompany me back into the room."

"I will go with you," said Susan.

Rebecca looked at Officer Jim as though she would have preferred him to come than a woman. Susan understood the look the doctor gave Officer Jim. He was about to speak until Susan gave him an evil look. When Rebecca realized Jim wasn't going to object to Susan going, she hunched her shoulders and smiled at Susan.

"Are you ready, Ma'am?"

Susan smiled and pointed toward the door.

"After you, Ma'am."

Rebecca smiled and walked back into the room. Susan followed her. Sherman sat on the stretcher with his back to the door. Nurse Rose was wrapping bandages around his head. Nurse Lou sat at the desk by the door filling out some papers. All of them looked over to the door when Rebecca and Susan entered the room. Susan and Sherman made eye contact but neither spoke. Rebecca spoke to Nurse Rose as she continued to bandage Sherman's head.

"How is the patient?" Rebecca asked.

Susan leaned on the door.

"He is fine," said Nurse Rose replied. "No broken bones."

Nurse Tom nodded his head in agreement.

"How do you feel, Mr. Ford?" Rebecca asked.

"I'm fine and I'm ready to return back to population," he said.

"I don't know about that," she said.

Sherman looked at Rebecca in disbelief.

"What!?" he snapped.

"I said, "I don't know if that will happen'," she said.

"What in the hell do you mean you don't know if that is going to happen?!" he demanded.

Susan stood up off of the door.

"Calm down, Mr. Ford!" she ordered.

Sherman glanced over at Susan and looked back at Rebecca. Nurse Rose was bandaging his waist and chest.

"Mr. Ford is fine except for his bruises. I told him he may experience a little aches and pains but he should be fine," Nurse Rose said, reassuringly.

"Mr. Ford," said Rebecca, "I have brought this nice correctional officer in to talk to you about what really happened to you."

Sherman was furious.

"Man, what the fuck are you talking about!!?" Sherman snapped.

Susan spoke as if she was angry.

"Mr. Ford! You will reframe from using that language and that tone of voice!! And I mean this!" Susan said as she pointed her finger at him.

Sherman looked at Susan like she was crazy. Her face was blood shot red. The medics in the room also looked at Susan. Rebecca placed her hand on Susan's shoulder and smiled at her.

"Ma'am, it's okay, I'm used to inmates becoming upset," Rebecca said, smiling.

Rebecca looked back at Sherman. He was still looking toward Susan.

"Mr. Ford, we are all here to help you and we want to help you. Allow us to help you," she said.

Sherman used the tips of his fingers from his left hand to wipe his eyes. He spoke in a calm voice.

"Doc, I told you what happened. I don't know what you believe happened, but what you believe did not happen," Sherman said.

Rebecca looked at Susan. She hunched her shoulders.

"Doc, there is nothing I can do. The man said he fell in the shower," Susan replied.

Rebecca rolled her eyes at Susan and looked back at Sherman.

"Mr. Ford, I really do hope nothing else happens to you," Rebecca said with concern.

"Now can I go?" Sherman replied.

Rebecca nodded her head.

"Yes, you may," Rebecca replied.

Sherman stood up and put his shirt on.

Nurse Rose stood in front of Sherman.

"Mr. Ford, I want you to take things light for a little while. No exercise, no sports and refrain from lifting any heavy objects," Nurse Rose asked, politely.

She smiled at Sherman.

"And be careful in the shower," Nurse Rose added.

Sherman returned a smile and extended his hand. The doctor firmly shook his hand.

"Thank you, Doc," he said.

Nurse Rose nodded her head.

"You are welcome and you will be fine. I will call you back down here in a few days to check your wounds and bruises. For now, I will give you some meds to take with you. It will help you with the pain. Okay, Mr. Ford?" Nurse Rose said.
Sherman nodded his head, "Okay, Doc."

Susan opened the door and Sherman came walking past her.

"Mr. Ford, place your hands on the wall in the hallway. I have to search you," Susan ordered.

Sherman looked at her like she was crazy.

"Yea, R-right," he said.

Sherman walked over to the wall. Susan closed the door behind her and walked over to him.

He was looking at her. Officer Jim was no longer sitting in his chair.

"Go ahead and put your hands on the wall," Susan pointed to the wall.

"What!? You were serious!?" he said.

Susan smiled.

"Yes. I was. I have to make it look good. You see the men in the waiting room," she asked him.

Sherman looked over to the waiting room. Men were pressed up against the fiberglass looking at them. Sherman looked at the walls and placed his hands on them the best he could. He grimaced the whole time.

"Do what you have to do," he said.

Susan patted him down. She ran her hands from his groin down his legs. Sherman and Susan both started smiling when the inmates yelled, "Check me!! I got something!! Fuck that!! I got a knife in my dip!!" Susan shook her head as she laughed. She stood up and Sherman turned around.

"Are you okay though?" she asked.

"Yea, I'm just sleepy," he replied.

"So I won't see you later?" she said, pouting.

"Nah, call me down tomorrow," Sherman replied.

"What happened to you?" she asked.

"I fell in the shower," he said without batting an eye.

"Yeah, right. Sherman, you don't trust me unless I have my clothes off," she said in disappointment.

"Look Susan, I'm tired. I'm just ready to get some rest," he said, impatiently.

Susan looked disappointed.

"Well, come on," she replied with irritation.

Susan followed Sherman over to the waiting room. She unlocked the door and the inmates exited the room. To her surprise, all of the inmates placed their hands on the wall. They all wanted to be searched. Susan held the back of her left hand over her mouth to hide her smile.

"I am not searching y'all," she exclaimed.

All of the inmates said, "Damn."

"Come on so y'all can go," she barked, humorously.

All of the men stood in a straight line. Sherman was in front of the line. Susan followed them to the entrance of their tier. When the gate opened, all of the men walked to the next gate. She stood beside the first gate. The first gate closed then the second gate opened, all of the men walked through the gate. Sherman stopped at John's cell. John was sitting on top of his bed with his back against the wall playing solitaire. Beside John's bed was a school desk with a brown towel on top of it.

There was a 16" color television on top of the desk and some empty tobacco cans adjacent to the television. Beside the desk was a five-foot metal

246

*tan locker. John looked up when Sherman stepped in
the doorway. He smiled when he saw his friend.*

"What's up, Playa!?" John asked.

Sherman returned a smile, "Nothing much."

*John got off his bed and stepped on top of
one of the four dark blue towels that was spread out
on his floor. He wore a white tank top and blue
cotton boxer shorts. He was bare foot. He walked
over to Sherman and shook his hand.*

"Damn, Sherman, I thought I wouldn't see you for a
while man. They have you all taped up," John said.

"John, ya didn't touch that dude did ya?" Sherman
questioned.
John shook his head.

"Nah, he came to me and Brace and tried to squash
the beef, but we told him that is ya beef. We don't
have shit to do with it. Then dude just walked off.
How are you feeling?" John said with concern.

"I'm okay, I'm just tired. So look, I'm going to get
some sleep. I will come down when I get up,"
Sherman replied.

"You sure you don't want me to get the dude?" John
said.

"I'm sure. I will handle that problem." Sherman
replied.

"R-right, whatever you say."

The two friends shook hands then Sherman walked slowly down to his cell, took his clothes off and went to sleep.

Chapter Eighteen

Sherman opened his eyes and stared at the wall that the bed was up against. He could feel someone watching him. By the time he rolled over to look at the cell door, he could see a human figure walk away. He threw the cover off of him and hurried up and put on his boots. He quickly tied up the boots and stood up. Then he lifted up his mattress and grabbed an eleven-inch shank. He tucked the knife away in his waist and pulled his red tank top over the knife. The knife slipped through his boxer short and fell onto the floor.

Sherman looked down at his waist and saw that he only wore boxer shorts. He picked the weapon up off the floor and put on his blue shorts. Sherman tucked the knife back into his waist and this time it stayed. He walked over to the bars and pulled back the door. He stepped onto the tier and looked to his left then right.

The tier was crowded with inmates but he didn't notice Brace, John, or Philly. He turned right and walked down the tier to the dayroom. He walked into the crowded dayroom and looked around at the men watching the football game on the color television.

Sherman spotted Philly leaning up against the wall. The man had his left foot on the wall as he leaned his back up against it. Philly had his right elbow on top of the last pay-phone, talking to another prisoner named Jeff.

Philly locked eyes with Sherman. He leaned up off of the wall and snatched his shank from his waist. Jeff froze in fear. He immediately thought he was going to stab him. Then Jeff noticed that Philly was staring at Sherman. Sherman pulled his shank from his waist and Philly started grinning.

All of the prisoners who were watching the football game quickly moved out of the way of the two men. Some of the prisoners briskly left the dayroom. Brace and John were two of the men in the room. They started creeping toward Philly as they eased their knives out of their waists. Sherman noticed them from the corner of his right eye.

"Chill out y'all! This is my night to shine!" Sherman shouted.

John and Brace both stopped in their tracks and just looked at Sherman. Both had their shanks gripped in their hands. Sherman's head and upper body was still heavily bandaged. Sherman just stared at Philly and said,

"Nigga, what the fuck's up!?"

Philly did not respond. He just spit to his left, hitting the wall. Jeff just stood there watching the two men.

Philly said to Jeff, " Won't you go over there with the others and watch me work."

Jeff did not respond. He just walked over to the other side of the room. John and Brace stared evilly at Jeff as Jeff moved away from them.

"Bitch, what are you waiting for!? Let's get it on!!" said Sherman.

"Nigga, I beat your bitch ass with a lock in a sock yesterday so now it's your move!" said Philly.

John walked over to Sherman.

"Here, Sherm," said John.

John handed Sherman his shank. Sherman held both of the knives gripped in his hand as he cautiously stepped toward Philly. He could hear his own heartbeat; it was so quiet after one of the men turned off the television. Sherman's throat was dry like sand. Philly moved strategically toward him, his knife still gripped in his hand, staring into Sherman's eyes.

"Get your man, Sherman!!" yelled Brace.

Philly swung his knife toward Sherman's head. Sherman leaned his upper body backwards to dodge the knife then with a quick thrust Sherman slashed him across his chest. Philly jumped back and looked down at his torn sweatshirt. Then he looked viciously at Sherman.

Brace and John were yelling in the background, "Kill that bitch, Sherman!!"

Philly took two steps toward Sherman as if he was about to charge him but then he kicked him in the chest instead. Sherman yelped in pain as he fell back into the crowd. The men pushed the grimacing Sherman back into the middle of the floor. He moved toward Philly swinging his right arm inwards but under. When Philly jumped backwards, Sherman brought his left arm downwards, cutting the man

251

across his chest near his right armpit. Philly jumped
backwards to avoid from being stabbed again.

"Kill that bitch!!" yelled Brace. "Cut his
motherfucking heart out!!"

John just stared as everyone else did at the
two men.

"I'm going to kill you!" said Philly. "You bitch!!"

Sherman smirked. Then Philly charged at him,
pushing his knife into Sherman's gut. Sherman yelled
in pain as he backed into the wall. Philly held the
knife in Sherman's gut twisting it. Sherman screamed
in agony then he jammed both of his knives through
Philly's ribs forcibly. Philly cried out in pure pain as
he looked up at the ceiling.

Brace moved swiftly over to the two men.
He grabbed Philly's right ear with his left hand and
swung his right hand and shank underneath the man's
neck. With the blade of his knife, he sliced Philly's
neck from his left ear around to his right ear. The
man's body started shaking uncontrollably as he fell
backwards into Brace's arms. Philly's blood gushed
out of his neck onto the wall and Sherman's face and
chest.

The other inmates could be heard moaning
at the disgusting scene. Brace stepped to the right
and allowed Philly's body to fall onto the concrete
floor. Philly's body continued to convulse until the
last drop of life exited him. His body laid still with
blood steadily running from the gash in his neck. A
lot of the other inmates including Jeff left the
dayroom. Sherman leaned up against the wall
holding his bleeding stomach, staring painfully at

Brace and John. Brace and John ran over to their friend.

Sherman spoke painfully, jokingly, "Man, how in the hell am I going to explain this?"

Both John and Brace smiled at him as they held him up.

"We will think of something," said Brace.

"Man, I want to sit down," said Sherman.

"Man," John stated, "I'm not allowing you to die on us."

"I'm not dying. I'm just in a lot of pain and I think it will slow the bleeding down if I sit down. Just let me slide down the wall," Sherman said smiling, "And I promise I won't die."

Brace and John helped Sherman sit down on the floor and leaned his back up against the wall. Pops, a black man with salt and pepper hair walked over to them. The man had a potbelly and he wore a light blue dress shirt and gray slacks.

"Do you young fellas want me to get the law so your friend will not bleed to death? Sitting on the floor ain't going to stop him from bleeding," said Pops.

John was kneeling down beside Sherman when he looked at the old man.

"Yea, that will work. Thanks, I will set you straight," John replied.

Pops waved the gesture off with his left hand.

"Don't bother. It has been a long time since I've seen real gladiators go at each other," Pops said as he looked at Sherman, "Young man, you did good."

Sherman smiled up at the man in agony.

"I will go now," said Pops.

The old man walked over to Philly's corpse and saw the knife sticking out of his side. He also noticed that the dead man's eyes were closed and he looked at peace. Pops looked over at the three men. Brace and John were both kneeling down beside Sherman talking to him.

"Hey, Young fellas!" yelled Pops.

Brace looked over toward him. Pops was pointing at the knife in the dead man's left rib.

"Ya better clean up before the law gets down here."

Brace nodded his head in agreement.

"Okay," said Brace

Pops then wobbled out of the dayroom. Sherman started talking, still in a lot of pain.

"Won't you two get the knives and get the fuck out of here. I got this," said Sherman.

John looked into Sherman's eyes like a caring father would his hurting son.

"Are you sure?" asked John.

Sherman nodded his head, closing his left eye because of the pain.
"Yea, I'm sure. Roll out," Sherman ordered.

John patted Sherman gently on his right foot and nodded his head.

"Okay," as John looked at Brace, he said, "R-right Brace, let's clean up and roll out."

Brace said, "Let's roll."

Both men picked up all of the weapons and walked over to the door. They both stopped at the door, looked over at Sherman before leaving.

A few seconds later, Corporal James, Corporal Kritz, and Corporal Raul ran into the dayroom with clubs in their hand. The officers looked at the pool of blood now around Philly's body, and then they looked at Sherman who was leaning up against the wall. Sherman's blood was also forming a pool. His red tank top turned crimson because of the blood leaking from his wound.

Corporal Kritz pulled out his walkie-talkie and called for the emergency medical team. Rebecca and the other nurses were in the dayroom in seconds. They strapped Sherman down on the stretcher and rushed him to the medical unit.

Later that same day, an ambulance drove Sherman to the local hospital. After he came out of the emergency room, he was placed in a hospital room surrounded by bars. Sherman laid in the bed with his right ankle shackled to one of the hospital bed's railing. Officer Jim sat in a green plastic chair outside of the bars. He had his back toward Sherman, listening to his iPod. Sherman lay in the bed with a white sheet covering him up to his waist. He had his left palm placed between the thick white pillow and his head. He just stared at the ceiling and then he looked toward Officer Jim.

"Hey C-O, " Sherman weakly shouted.

Sherman said in a mild tone of voice. The guard did not respond.

"Hey C-O!" he shouted again.

Officer Jim still did not hear Sherman's voice. The music from the earphones muffled out all sound except the music being played. The guard was nodding his head to the beat of the music.

"Bitch ass nigga! You hear me calling your motherfucken ass!! H-E-Y Cee-Ohh!!" Sherman yelled.

This time the guard heard him yelling. He pulled the earphones off of his ears and looked back over at Sherman. He spoke in an unfriendly but nonthreatening tone.

"Did you say something?" asked Officer Jim.

Sherman was very upset.

"Yea, bitch ass nigga, if you wouldn't of had those motherfucking earphones on, you would of heard me calling your sorry ass!! Now get the fuck over here!" Sherman barked.

Sherman was serious. The guard just shook his head and grinned as he looked at Sherman. Then Officer Jim spoke in a calm voice.

"Man, I do not know who the hell you think you are talking to, so I'm getting ready to put these earphones back on my ears," Officer Jim barked, "When you want to call me in a respectful manner, my name is, Corporal or Officer Jim."

That is exactly what the guard did as he turned back around. Sherman looked to his right. There was a desk beside his bed with a plastic brown cup on it. He slowly reached over and grabbed the cup. He looked into the full cup of water and mumbled:

"This nigga don't know who he is fucking with."

Sherman grimaced as he tossed the cup at the cage. Some of the water spilled on Sherman as he threw it. When the cup crashed into the cage, the rest of the water poured onto the guard. Officer Jim jumped up out of his chair and grabbed the back of his neck as if he was wounded. After he saw that it was water on his palms, he looked insanely at Sherman's smiling face.

"You motherfucking punk!" Officer Jim shouted

Sherman busted into laughter and grimaced as he held his painful side.

"I thought you were thirsty. Did you get enough?" Sherman asked smiling.

Officer Jim was so angry that he struggled to pull his keys off of his belt. Once he got the key ring off his belt, he went and unlocked the cage door. As he walked toward Sherman he mumbled.

"I'm going to whip your ass, you punk," Officer Jim threatened.

He raised both of his fists in the air in preparation to punch Sherman. Sherman stared at him in wonder as he walked closer to him. Officer Jim froze when he heard the female's voice.

"Is everything okay in here?" asked Nurse Tyree.

Officer Jim turned sideways and looked at the beautiful small-framed black woman. She stood in the doorway of the cage wearing an all white nurses' uniform. She had beautiful tan skin and shoulder length black hair.

"Is everything okay in here?" she said with a look of suspicion.

The nurse's question was directed to Sherman but Officer Jim smiled at her and said:

"Yes, Ma'am."

"Sherman spoke in a playful voice, "I m okay but I think this stupid guard is insane. I'm sure glad you came because I think the guard was about to get himself hurt up in here."

Officer Jim stared sinisterly at Sherman. Nurse Tyree walked over to the guard.

"Excuse me, Officer," she said as she gestured with her eyes for him to leave.

"Yes, Ma'am," said Officer Jim, as he walked over to the exit.

He looked at Sherman for a second then she looked at him. He went and sat down in his chair.

Nurse Tyree spoke, "Mr. Ford, lift your head up so I can fluff up your pillow."

Sherman did as he was told as she fluffed the pillow. He then laid his head back on it still smiling. She just looked at him.

"Are you in here causing trouble?" she said in a playful tone.

"Never," Sherman responded.

She started smiling because she knew Sherman was lying. Then she looked at Sherman seriously.

"How do you feel?" she asked.

Sherman looked and answered her question seriously.

"I am fine. Thank you for asking," Sherman said, smiling.

"Does your stomach feel sour, tight, and thumping?" she asked.

"Nah," said Sherman.

Nurse Tyree started smiling.

"Well prepare yourself because it will when those drugs wear off. Call me when it starts to bother you," she said.

Sherman spoke smiling, "Can I call you when it doesn't?"

The nurse knew he was flirting with her so she blushed and said, "No."

Nurse Tyree pointed to the call button that resembled a remote control with a long white cord that ran from the object to somewhere behind the bed.

"Whenever you feel the pain starting, push the blue button," she said.

She turned and walked out of the room. Officer Jim locked the cage door back. Sherman folded his arms and went to sleep.

Chapter Nineteen

U.S. Marshall Gibbs, a tall muscular Black man with a tan suit, matching tie, Kangol hat and a white shirt stood by the head of Sherman's bed. Marshall Gibbs was accompanied by U.S. Marshall Diamante a muscular white man with reddish hair and a mustache. Marshall Diamante wore an all blue suit and tie and a white shirt. He stood at the foot of Sherman's bed. Sherman laid sound asleep on his back with his hands folded across the sheet on top of his chest. Marshall Gibbs leaned over near Sherman's right ear and whispered.

"Mr. Ford. Wake up, Mr. Ford," said Marshall Gibbs.

Sherman peeped out of his right eye and with a smirk on his face said.

"Man, who the fuck are you?"

Sherman stuck his left index finger in his left ear and scratched it. He wiped his finger on the sheet. He glanced down at U.S. Marshall Diamante. Then he looked U.S. Marshall Gibbs straight in his eyes.

"Man, who the fuck are y'all," Sherman demanded.

U.S. Marshall Gibbs stood with his right hand in his jacket pocket.

"I'm U.S. Marshall Gibbs, and that is U.S. Marshall Diamante."

*Sherman pushed his upper body on top of
the pillow and sat half way up.*

"So what the fuck are y'all looking in my face for!"

*U.S. Marshall Gibbs now looked at Sherman
with an unfriendly smirk.*

"Mr. Ford, you will refrain from using that
unnecessary language," U.S. Marshall Gibbs said.

*Sherman looked at Marshall Gibbs and
started grinning.*

"Or what?" Sherman said.

*U.S. Marshall Gibbs pulled his right hand
out of his jacket pocket and shook his index finger
angrily at Sherman. He wore a gold pinky ring with a
black onyx in the middle. The ceiling light sparkled
off the ring.*

"Or I will kick your ass in here! Now you decide!!"
U.S. Marshall Gibbs shouted.

*Sherman saw that U.S. Marshall Gibbs was
in a rage. The Marshall's dark beady brown eyes
stared evilly into his eyes. He saw a US Marshall
beat a man half to death when he was in the bullpen
at the courthouse. So he knew the man was not
making a threat, but a promise. Sherman knew he
was in no shape to be fighting these two Hulk Hogan
sized men. He decided to take the bass out of his
voice as he spoke.*

"Man, what do you want?"

*U.S. Marshall Gibbs placed both of his
hands in his jacket pockets. He had a little smile on*

his face, as he knew that Sherman knew they would kick his ass.

"Mr. Ford, we are here to ask you a few questions about the stabbing you were involved in."

Sherman just nodded his head in agreement.

"Mr. Ford, what happened?" U.S. Marshall Gibbs asked.

"Me and my friend were watching the football game, then all of a sudden we were attacked from behind. I think my friend was killed. Luckily, I survived," Sherman said, innocently.

"So Mr. Reed was your friend?" U.S. Marshall Gibbs asked.

Sherman was not sure who Mr. Reed was but he was hoping it was the dead man.

"Yes, is he dead?" Sherman asked with concern.

Sherman looked saddened. Marshall Gibbs nodded his head and looked apologetic.

"Yes, I am afraid Mr. Reed is no longer with us," said U.S. Marshall Gibbs.

Sherman looked down at his folded hands and shook them sorrowfully. Then he looked up at the ceiling. He looked as if he was about to start crying and was trying to fight off tears.

"Damn," Sherman said, tearfully, "that was my partner."

"Mr. Ford, I'm sorry... But we have to ask you some more questions," said U.S. Marshall Diamante.

Sherman sniffed as if he was still trying to fight off the tears. He looked up at U.S. Marshall Gibbs.

"Ask me what you want," Sherman said.

"Mr. Ford, did you see who stabbed you and killed your friend?" U.S. Marshall Diamante asked.

Sherman shook his head side to side.

"No, I think it was a pillowcase that was thrown over my head."

"So you don't have any idea about who may have done this to you?" U.S. Marshall Diamante responded.

Sherman shook his head side to side again.

"No. The only people that I know of that don't like me is the Aryan Brotherhood or the Hispanics. But then again, they wouldn't have tried to kill us in a dayroom full of blacks."

"Mr. Ford, I was told you were beaten with a heavy object a few days ago? That's why there are bandages on your head, right?" U.S. Marshall Diamante asked.

Sherman shook his head side to side.

"No... that's not true, I fell in the shower. The doctors at the prison started that rumor. But it is not true," Sherman replied.

"Okay Mr. Ford, we'll be leaving now. But if you find out who did this to you and your friend, notify the personnel at the institution," U.S. Marshall Diamante said with concern.

"I will," Sherman said.

U.S. Marshall Gibbs walked over to the cage door. U.S. Marshall Diamante smiled at Sherman and walked over to the cage door beside his partner and they left.

Sherman laid back down and placed both of his palms under his head and closed his eyes. He smiled at his achievement of fooling the U.S. Marshalls and went back to sleep.

"Hey, Boo," Susan whispered.

Sherman opened his eyes and to his surprise saw Susan. She looked extremely worried. He unknowingly had a big smile on his face. She was smiling down at him, her hazel eyes were glowing and she wore bright red lipstick.

"Damn, what the fuck are you doing here?" Sherman smiled happily.

Susan started giggling.

"I talked my boss into letting me work over here. I was so scared when I heard what happened to you. Are you all right?" she said with a look of gloom.

Sherman knew Susan loved him and that she was concerned about him. He nodded his head and smiled.

"Yea, I'm fine."

Susan still looked sad.

"Boo, somebody is trying to kill you. Please, check in," she pleaded.

Sherman could not believe what he heard. He was struck with anger. His facial expression turned from a smile to grit.

"What the fuck did you just tell me to do?!" he snapped.

She looked at him with shock and surprise.

"I'm sorry, I'm just scared, S-h-e-r man," she pleaded.

Sherman still spoke with anger but in a lower tone of voice.

"Man, I am alright. Why in the hell do you keep taking these risks to see me?" he demanded.

"Cause," she said, trying to look away.

" Cause what?" Sherman demanded.

"Cause I care about you and I worry about you," Susan said as she nervously toyed with her hands.

Sherman just shook his head in disbelief.

"Shorty, you are a weird broad," he said, shaking his head.

Susan smiled.

"Boy..." she said.

"Did the jail notify my people about what happened?" he asked.

Susan's facial expression turned to a smirk and she rolled her eyes.

"Yea, they called your baby's mother and she came down here but they could not allow her to see you," Susan replied.

"Why?" Sherman demanded.

Susan let her resentment out as she spoke in almost a yell.

"Why you keep asking me about her!?" Susan said with irritation.

Sherman tilted his head to the right as he gritted on Susan and spoke with disbelief.

"What!? That's my motherfucking daughter's mother! What you forgot, I ain't your motherfucking man!" he shouted.

Susan closed her eyes and let out a deep breath. She then turned and walked out of the cage. She locked the cage and flopped down in her chair. She folded her arms across her chest and crossed her legs. Sherman looked angrily at her back. She rocked in her seat. His facial expression turned into a sad frown because he knew he had hurt her feelings. He knew she was only mad because she loved him and wanted to be his one and only girl.

"Hey Susan!" he said in a sorrowful tone.

Susan did not respond but she stopped shaking.

"Hey S-u-san!" he said in a singing voice.

Susan yelled back at him without turning to look at him.

"What!!?"

"Girl, come here!!" he said, smiling.

Susan spoke still not looking at Sherman.

"For what!? So you can hurt my damn feelings again!!?"

Sherman let out a deep breath and lowered his voice.

"Susan, can you please come here?" he said.

She tossed her body out of the chair like she did not want to go. She walked over to the cage and unlocked the door and walked over to him with the left side of her lip balled up. She spoke in a girlish voice.

"What do you want?" she said, blushing.

Sherman smiled. She could not help but to smile. She started giggling then she gently hit Sherman across his arm.

"Boy, don't make me laugh. I'm mad," she said, smiling

"Girl, you ain't mad," he said, smiling.

Susan shook her head as she smiled and spoke.

"Yes I am. You hurt my feelings," she said folding her arms across her chest.

Sherman looked Susan seriously in her eyes causing her smile to freeze.

"I didn't mean to hurt your feelings. Susan, you just have to understand, my baby's mother is my family," he said.

She looked sad as she looked down at his hands as he scratched his wrist.

"I know. I should not be getting you mad. You told me from the beginning you had a girlfriend," she confessed.

Sherman took his right hand and grabbed her right hand and caressed the back of it with his thumb.

"Susan, I really do got it in for you. I really do. And I really appreciate your concern for me," he said, reassuringly.

She rocked side to side as she blushed.

"Excuse me," interrupted Nurse Tyree.

Susan looked to her left and there was a short black nurse standing beside her. Susan smiled at her. Nurse Tyree faked a smile back. Susan looked at Sherman and walked out of the room.
Nurse Tyree stared angrily into Sherman's eyes, and nodded her head toward Susan.

"What's up with the white girl?" she asked.

Sherman started smiling. From the nurse's facial expression, he knew she was dead serious.

"Ain't shit, why you ask?" he said, nonchalantly.

"Girlfriend hanging all over you like she's your girl," said the nurse. "What's up?"

Sherman giggled.

"Shorty, you're lunchen. But what's up?"

"It's time for you to go, you have just been released back to the prison," said Nurse Tyree.

Sherman looked disappointed. He had a smirk on his face as he shook his head and looked at the nurse.

"Damn, I didn't even get a chance to kiss you," he said, smiling.

She rolled her eyes at him and spoke with her left hand on her hip.

"Boy please, you better try and fuck that white girl, 'cause you don't have nothing coming here," she said, half jokingly.

Two large white male prison guards walked into the room. The nurse and Sherman looked at the two men. One of the guards spoke.

"Miss, can we take him now?"

Nurse Tyree nodded her head in agreement.

"Yes, you sure can," Nurse Tyree responded.

The other guard pulled some shackles off of his belt. He used a handcuff key to unlock the shackles that had Sherman's right leg cuffed to the bed. Sherman got up and sat on the edge of the bed. The guard with the shackles stooped down and placed the shackles around Sherman's ankle. Nurse Tyree leaned up against the wall looking at them. Once both shackles were on his ankles, the guard held Sherman's left arm gently while he stood up. Sherman wearing only a hospital gown had a smirk on his face. Then the other guard pulled a long chain from off his belt and wrapped it around Sherman's waist.

"Shit!" said the guard, "I forgot to cuff him first."

Sherman shook his head thinking to himself, "This dude is stupid." The guard pulled the chain from around Sherman's waist and placed it on his shoulder. He then took a pair of handcuffs out of a pouch and handcuffed Sherman. Sherman let his arms rest against his leg. The guard wrapped the chain back around Sherman's waist and hooked the black box around the handcuff chain.

Next the guard hooked the waist chain to the box. Sherman sat down on the edge of the bed. One of the guards placed a pair of hospital shoes on Sherman's feet and told him to follow them out. The other guard, nurse, and Susan all followed.

There were *eight other cages like the one Sherman was in on this wing of the hospital. When Sherman got to the second cage, he stopped, as he thought he saw someone he knew. Walking to the cage, the officer on duty in front of the cage said:*

"What are you doing?"

The guard Sherman was following turned around to look at Sherman. Sherman placed his hands on the cage smiling, not paying the guard any attention and shouted with cheer in his voice.

"Hey KT! KT!" Nigga, its Sherman!"

KT laid on his bed with his eyes closed as if he was asleep. When Sherman called KT's name, he was motionless. Sherman used his knee to bang on the cage, still smiling.

"Hey KT! Nigga, get up!" Sherman shouted.

KT still did not respond. Sherman did not notice all of the wires connected to KT. The guard who was sitting walked over to Sherman and yelled.

"Get out of here!"

Sherman looked the guard evilly in his eyes then looked back at KT's still body. He then spotted that all of the cords hooked up to KT's chest and face were attached to a breathing machine. He looked at Nurse Tyree. She stood beside him and tried to comfort him by gently caressing his shoulder.

"What's wrong with my main man?" Sherman pleaded.

Nurse Tyree looked into Sherman's eyes and saw how much he really cared for KT. She knew what she was about to tell him would be devastating.

"I'm sorry, but your friend is brain dead," she said.

Sherman closed his eyes and let out a deep breath then looked back into her eyes.

"He's a vegetable?" Sherman asked.

The nurse nodded her head and in a sorrowful voice and said:

"I'm afraid so. He has been that way for months. His family does not want to allow him to die but he's really already dead."

Sherman's eyes filled with tears. Susan wanted to go and hug him so bad but she couldn't. She bit down on her lip to stop her urges to hug him and to fight her tears. The other two guards walked over to Sherman.

"Let's go," Mr. Ford.

"I'm sorry," said the nurse

Sherman looked at the nurse and the guard then he walked off. They escorted Sherman back to The Hill where he stayed in the medical unit for two weeks. While in the medical unit, he had sex with Susan twice. On the fourteenth day Sherman was sent back to his cell.

Chapter Twenty

Sherman walked through the gate that led to the prison yard. His eyes bounced around at some of the three hundred inmate's faces. It was a windy and cold day. So the inmates all wore either heavy prison coats, coats from home, or thick sweat hoods with insulated hats. Sherman wore his thick brown Eddie Bauer coat and brown insulated hat. He had both of his hands inside his upper coat pockets. He looked over to the weight area beside the bleachers, looking for Brace or John. A lot of other prisoners were lifting weights. Sherman looked up toward the bleachers and still did not see his buddies. He then looked toward the track and spotted Brace and John walking around the track. He pulled his hood over his head and walked up behind them. He placed his hands on their shoulders. Both men looked curiously at him. When they noticed Sherman, they both started smiling. John reached over his own shoulder and shook Sherman's right hand.

"What's up, Playa?" asked John.

"Nothing at all...." said Sherman. "It's cold out this mother though."

"Sure is," said Brace.

Sherman and Brace shook hands, Brace pointed up to Sherman's head.

"How is the head?" Brace asked

"It's wrapped up and healing... Oh yea, we're cool on that beef," Sherman replied.

Sherman referred to the stabbing in the dayroom.

"That's cool. So how's the stomach, too? Fuck it," Brace said, laughing, "How is your health?"

"Man, I'm cool. How the hell is your health?"

Brace stopped smiling. To Sherman it seemed like everything just stopped moving, even the wind stopped blowing. Sherman put his hands back inside of his upper coat pocket and looked at Brace. He was just staring straight ahead as they walked.

"Man, what's up?" asked Sherman.

Brace never stopped looking straight ahead. He didn't even blink.

"Man, the doctors told me I got that shit," Brace confessed.

"What shit?" Sherman asked.

Brace stopped walking and looked Sherman straight in his eyes.

"HIV," Brace said.

Sherman looked at the ground and shook his head.

"Damn!"

Sherman looked back at Brace.

"Are they sure?" Sherman questioned.

"I hope not. They took more blood to test it again. But I know I got that shit because I can feel the changes in my body," Brace said.

He looked into Sherman's eyes and said,

"Let's leave that shit alone, let's talk about something else."

"R-right," Sherman replied.

The three men started walking again in silence. They walked all the way around the track without saying a word. John pointed over to two men by the weights. They were body punching.

"Look at those fools," said John, "Come on y'all! Watch them get serious."

"Man, fuck those niggas," said Brace.

"Man, I'm tired of walking around the track anyway," said John.

"Well, come on then," Brace said.

As the three men walked toward the two men who were boxing, one of the boxers slipped and hit the other man in the mouth. The man immediately grabbed his mouth as he bent forward in pain. The other man started apologizing as he laughed. The injured man removed his hand from his mouth and saw the blood on his hand. His sparring partner apologized again but continued to laugh as he held up his palm. The injured man gave him a high five. As he walked over to his jacket near the wall, the other man started throwing punches at the air in the opposite direction.

Sherman and his crew leaned against the wall, watching the man shadow boxing. The injured man walked up behind the shadow boxer and started stabbing him in his upper back. The man stumbled forward almost falling but he caught his grip. He spun around and seemed surprised to see the other man charging at him with the knife. He was stabbed this time in the side of his face. He spun around with great speed and started to run away. His attacker chased him across the field stabbing him a few more times. Finally, the man who was being stabbed jumped on the barb wire fence and started climbing it. His attacker dived to the ground after two gunshots rang out. The man on the fence crashed to the ground. Dead.

All of the inmates ducked or laid on the ground. A man's voice yelled over the intercom, "Lay down!! All of you!! Lay down now!!" The prisoners did as they were told. A few seconds later about twenty two guards ran on the field armed with shields, guns and metal helmets. They handcuffed the stabber. Then three guards escorted him out of the yard. Some of the other guards walked over to the dead man by the fence. His shirt was crimson with two bullet holes in his back.

The other prisoners remained on their stomachs on the ground. One of the guards spoke into his walkie-talkie, seconds later, the same male voice screamed through the intercom, "All inmates report back to your cells now!! The prison is now on lockdown." All of the inmates started getting up off the ground and heading to the exit. Sherman, Brace and John brushed themselves off. A medium built, *brown skinned man walked over to John and extended his hand.*

"What's up, John?" asked Tim.

John just stared at the man, not recognizing him with the dark blue hood and hat on his head. Then Tim pulled his hat and hood off. John's face lit up with a smile as he shook his hand and hugged him.

"What's up, Baby boy?" asked John.

They hugged again as they started laughing.

"Ain't shit!" said Tim.

"When did you get over here!?" asked John.

"Last night," Tim replied.

Sherman and Brace just stared at Tim in wonder. Sherman and Tim stared at each other then both men reached in their waist to pull out their knives. John and Brace noticed them. Brace grabbed Sherman by the lower part of his arm; John did the same to Tim. John looked at Tim then at Sherman while he was still holding Tim.

"What's up?, " asked John, "What's going on here?"

Sherman was gritting on the man.

"That's that bitch ass nigga who robbed me for my shoes!" Sherman shouted.

Tim started frowning at Sherman.

"Bitch nigga, I took that!" Tim barked.

Tim looked at Sherman's boots.

"Bitch, what size boots are those you got on!?" Brace said, sarcastically.

Sherman started trying to pull his shank out again.

"Bitch, they your size!" Sherman replied.

"Won't y'all chill out!!" John said.

"Man, I'm going to kill that nigga," said Sherman.

"Bitch, you ain't going to do shit," said Tim, "but take those boots off! Bitch ass nigga!"

Sherman looked Brace straight in his eyes and in a calm voice he spoke.

"Brace, let me go, Man. You hear this nigga." Sherman said.

"Man, I'm going to let you go," said Brace, "but chill out."

"Yea, R-right." Sherman said.

Brace pulled his hands away from Sherman hesitantly. John did the same.

"Chill out, Tim," said John.

Tim blew air from his mouth.

"John, I'm not trippin' off that chump," Tim replied.

Sherman looked at Tim.

"What!!?" Tim said, teasing.

Sherman took one step toward John and Tim before Brace grabbed him again.

"Chill out, Sherm," said Brace.

Sherman bit down on his lip and let out a deep breath as he stared evilly at Tim. Tim grabbed his groin and shook it as he talked.

"Man, that nigga is a chump." Tim said with humor.

With quick speed, Sherman moved passed Brace and punched Tim twice in his face. Tim stumbled backwards, but caught his grip. By the time Tim shook his head, Sherman was in front of him hitting him numerous times in his face and body. Tim managed to throw a few punches back at Sherman before John pulled them apart. Brace grabbed Sherman around his waist. John grabbed Tim around his arms and held him back.

"Man, that bitch swung on me!" said Tim.

"Nigga, you lucky I didn't put that knife in your ass!!" said Sherman.

"You should have!!" said Tim. "Nigga, you're mine!"

Other prisoners stood around looking at them. Three guards came between them. One of the guards yelled at them.

"What are you fuckers doing!? Didn't you hear the intercom!!?"

The guard pointed his stick toward the exit.

"Get your asses out of here now!!"

Sherman, John, Tim and Brace looked at the man like he was crazy. Then they walked out of the gate. John and Tim walked a few paces behind Sherman and Brace. Sherman kept looking back at Tim. Tim just smiled at him.

"Man, that bitch ass nigga think I'm a joke. I'mma kill that nigga, Brace!" Sherman confided.

Sherman looked back at Tim. Tim was talking to John and didn't see Sherman looking at him. Brace tugged on Sherman's coat. He turned around and looked forward while they walked.

"So that dude robbed you, Sherm?" asked Brace.

"Yea that joker robbed me. That nigga and his boy robbed me when I first got off the bus at Occoquan. Some youngens and I got his man before I could get at him. But that nigga there is mine... Why in the fuck did John interfere?" asked Sherman.

"It appears they know each other. You know John is with you one hundred percent, so follow his lead on this one." said Brace.

"Man, I ain't letting that shit slide!" Sherman barked.

"You don't suppose to, we just have to have a talk with John and see what's up." Brace said.

Sherman and Brace stopped and stood in the entrance of the building when Tim and John stepped into the building. John looked at Sherman then he stood in front of Tim.

"Sherman, chill out," said John.

"Man, what's up, John?" asked Sherman. "That is that same dude we were going to go after. Man, that chump robbed me. Let me and that bama settle our beef right here".

"Nigga, we can do just that!" yelled Tim.

Sherman pulled his knife from his waist. John stuck his palm out.

"Hold up, Man... Y'all niggas need to squash this beef!" said John.

"Man, fuck that nigga, John! Watch out," said Tim. "This won't take long."

"Yeah, let that bitch go," said Sherman. "It won't take long just like he said."

"Nah," said John, "I'm not letting y'all go out like that."

"John, let them go," Brace said. "They got a beef."

John shook his head side to side.

"Nah, Fuck that!..." said John, "Y'all going to squash that."

"Yea, whatever, John," said Sherman.

"Sherm, put the shank away, Police are coming down the hall." John said.

Sherman put the shank away as all four men watched Corporal James and Corporal Kritz head toward them. The prisoners that stood around

watching Sherman and Tim started walking off.
Other prisoners were still coming through the door
from outside. The two guards stopped beside the four
men. Then one of the guards spoke.

"What's the problem?" Corporal James said.

>*He looked at each man's face.*

"Man, ain't no motherfucking problem," said John.

>*Corporal James looked directly at John.*

"Well, I suggest you get your asses to your cells, as
you were told!" yelled the guard.

>*Corporal James then looked at Brace.*

"You sleep on the second floor, right?" Corporal
James demanded.

"No. On the first floor," answered Brace.

"Well, Bye," said Corporal James as he stepped
within inches of Brace's nose.

>*Brace gritted on him then walked through*
the open gate. Corporal James looked at Tim.

"Where do you live?"

"I sleep in cell two forty nine" said Tim with a frown
on his face.

"See you," said Corporal James as he waved his
fingers bye to him.

>*Tim turned to face John and they shook*
hands and embraced.

"Holla at you, Playa," said Tim.

"R-right," said John.

Tim looked at Sherman and started grinning. Then he walked through the open gate.

"Where do you two sleep?" Corporal James snapped at John and Sherman.

"On the first floor," said Sherman.

"First floor," said John.

Corporal James took his left hand and waved at them.

"Bye-bye."

John shook his head as he smiled. John and Sherman both turned and walked through the open gate.

"Sherman, let that shit go," said John.

"Man that dude took from me. He robbed me, John. C'mon man, he took my shoes. John, you know you wouldn't let that go," Sherman said, half jokingly.

"Trust me on this one. I need both of ya to let that shit go," John replied.

Sherman looked at John in disbelief.

"Man, if you didn't know the dude, you would be willing to destroy him *for* me," Sherman protested.

"True, but I *do* know the dude. Tim is a good dude. You just have to get to know him," John replied with hope.

Sherman stopped walking and turned toward John. He had both of his hands in his upper jacket pocket. John also stopped walking.

"Get to know him?" Sherman laughed and looked up at the ceiling, "That dude robbed me and threatened my life and you talking about getting to know him. I'm going to get to know him, when I put this knife in his neck."

"Don't go there," said John, "I'm asking you as a friend to leave that shit alone."

Sherman tilted his head to the left as he looked John in his eyes.
"Oh, what? Are you going to go against me if I kill that dude?" Sherman replied.

"That's not going to happen! I just want you to end the beef for me. Sherman, you know I don't ask you to do much for me on the strength of our friendship. I'm asking you to do this one thing for me. Let that shit go... Come on let's walk," said John.

They both started walking up the tier.

"If you let it go, Tim won't say shit else," John promised.

"John, man, I fuck with you from the heart. You like a brother to me but the dude robbed me and took what I owned," Sherman replied.

"I know... Damn, Sherman," John said with disappointment.

"'Damn, Sherman', what?" Sherman asked.

"The dude is cool. I just wish you would do what I ask this one time," John pleaded.

Sherman did not say anything. He and John both walked up to Brace's cell. Brace was standing behind locked bars. Other inmates were still on the tier.

"John, you know you supposed to step back and let Sherman and dude handle their beef," said Brace.

"Brace, man," said John, "I don't want them going at each other."

"I can understand that, but you weren't robbed. Sherman and dude are grown men. They can handle their problems," said Brace.

Sherman and John looked up the tier when they heard some commotion. They saw two prisoners stab another man. The man broke out running then collapsed. John and Sherman looked back at Brace.

"Well, that was our cue to leave," said John.

John shook Brace's hand through the bars.

"What happened? I can't see it," asked Brace.

"Some dude just caught the knife," said Sherman.

Sherman shook Brace's hand.

"See you tomorrow, Brace."
"R-right. See ya."

John and Sherman started walking down the steps. John stopped at his cell and turned to Sherman. The two men shook hands.

"I'll holla at you when we come off lockdown," said John.

"R-right," said Sherman."

John walked in his cell and closed the bars. Sherman proceeded down the tier. He looked at the unconscious man and kept on walking. He went into his cell and closed the bars. They stayed on lockdown for two days. The guards searched all of the cells. Guards found two knives in Brace's cell and locked him up. They also found a few knives in other prisoners' cells and locked them up as well.

Chapter Twenty-One

When the cell door opened, Sherman rolled out of bed. He put his boots on his feet and stood up. He wore a light blue shirt and a white tank top. He grabbed his washcloth and toothbrush off of the desk beside his bed and walked over to the sink. He pushed the faucet button but no water came out. Sherman tried to flush the toilet but it wouldn't flush. He looked down at the bed spread he has covering the toilet.

"Damn! It's been two days and the damn water isn't back on yet!" Sherman shouted.

Sherman then went and put his washcloth and toothbrush back on the desk.

There was an announcement over the intercom. "There will be no water today, Gentleman, but you are now off of lockdown."

Sherman could hear a lot of other inmates screaming, cursing, and yelling at the announcement. He walked over his cell bars and pulled the door back. He stepped onto the tier and looked to his left. He could see a lot of the inmates walking toward The Bubble. He then walked back into his cell and over to one of his lockers. He tilted the locker against the wall and pulled one of the four knives from under the locker. He stuck the knife between his shorts. Sherman then exited the cell, closing the door behind him.

There were over two dozen inmates in front of The Bubble. They were angrily shouting. The guards were angrily arguing and gesturing at the inmates from inside of The Bubble. Sherman noticed the commotion but didn't pay it any attention. He walked down the tier and up the steps. The second floor was filled with inmates shouting at The Bubble and talking amongst themselves. Then one prisoner came out of his cell and started throwing bars of soap at The Bubble. The prisoners in front of The Bubble quickly got out of the way as other prisoners from all of the tiers joined in and started throwing all kinds of small to medium size objects over the railings.

Sherman walked past some of the prisoners, not saying a word to them. Then he stopped and leaned his back up against the wall between two cells. Some of the prisoners looked at him curiously trying not to stare at him. Sherman peeped into the cell to his right. He came up off the wall and stood in front of the cell looking into it. He walked over to the rail and looked down at the crowd of men who were arguing with Corporal James and Corporal Kritz who were standing outside of The Bubble. Other prisoners started pulling their mattresses onto the tier and setting them on fire. Burning objects were falling down past Sherman from the tiers above. A short curly haired Mexican walked up and leaned on the rail beside Sherman. Sherman glanced over at the man and then looked back at the guards. The Mexican was looking at Sherman.

"Hey Migo," the Mexican said to Sherman.

Sherman looked at the Mexican frowning but did not say a word. The Mexican pointed down at the crowd by The Bubble.
"What's going on down there?" the man asked Sherman.

A white man who was leaning on the rail on the other side of Sherman, spoke.

"Shit is getting ready to hit the roof about the water being off."

Two more guards came out of the booth leaving the door open. There was another guard in the booth. The two guards started pushing the prisoners back. Then the prisoners started hitting the guards with their fists. Some of the prisoners could be seen pulling out knives. The guard's screams were muffled out by all of the noise the prisoners were making. The prisoners began stabbing the guards viciously. When the guard in the booth went to go close the door, three prisoners brandishing knives, ran inside the booth. Sherman noticed that one of the prisoners pushing his way inside of The Bubble was John. He could see the guard had fallen to the floor and the prisoners jabbing their knives into him.

Sherman then noticed Tim stumping Corporal Kritz as he lay down on the floor outside The Bubble. Corporal Kritz was trying to cover his body with his hands. Sherman turned and walked back down the steps.

Near the dayroom door, four or five inmates were beating another prisoner with their fists. Sherman moved passed them. As he went down the tier, he noticed other prisoners unconscious lying on the floor. Some inmates held bloody towels to their heads. Some inmates were bleeding from their faces, backs, heads, legs and arms. The whole scene looked like a combat zone. Sherman walked on past the men.

Corporal James ran past Sherman with about forty inmates chasing him. Sherman turned around to watch the inmates chase the guard. He saw one inmate run up beside Corporal James. The *guard swung at the man as he ran. Then the inmate tackled him onto the floor. The other inmates ran over to the guard and started kicking and hitting both men. Sherman started smiling and turned around as he headed down toward The Bubble. He spotted Tim still kicking the unconscious guard insanely. Sherman pulled his knife from his waist and held it gripped in his palm. He walked up behind Tim and wrapped his left arm tightly around Tim's neck and jammed his knife into the man's back. Tim let out a loud roar as Sherman forcefully ripped the blade up his back toward his neck.*

Sherman mumbled in Tim's ear, "Welcome to The Hill, Bitch."

When Tim's body began to shake, Sherman ripped the knife up another three inches. As Tim's eyes closed, Sherman felt a cold object push through his flesh. He could not scream because the person held him tightly by his Adam's apple as he pushed the knife deeper. Sherman tried to use his left hand to grab the cold object but when the person ripped the knife forcefully up Sherman's back, he dropped his hands to his side. He felt the blood pouring out of his back where the knife was still being held. He could feel his body growing weak and his sight fading. He tilted his head to his right to see who his killer was. He was even more shocked when he saw John holding him and biting down on his lip. He felt the knife push into his heart and he heard John whisper in his ear, "I'm sorry Sherman, but that was my brother." Then Sherman's eyesight went blank...

THE END.

Serving-N-Time

Serving-N-Time is a pen pal company owned by Lamont Carey in support of connecting caring individuals with prisoners. Currently, there are over two million prisoners incarcerated. Over 85% of prisoners will be released one day. Our goal is to assist you in connecting and encouraging them through correspondence. Prison is a lonely and depressing place. It can completely break a person's spirit and leave them angry with the world. Rehabilitation has to begin at the core of the person and prisons don't take on this responsibility proactively. It is up to us, the society, that these individuals will return to by assisting them in changing and spending their time preparing themselves for release and living productive lives after prison. We don't want them to end up like K.T., Gangster, Brace, John, or Sherman.

Prisoners can change. I did.

It just takes a willing individual and a caring community to change a life. Do you care enough to make our world a better place by equipping people who have made mistakes with the decision making skills that you possess?

If you are interested, go to: www.servingntime.com and choose a prisoner to write today. Their picture and contact information is posted on the site.

If you are a prisoner that is looking for a way to connect with people who want you to succeed, contact us at:

Serving-N-Time
P.O. Box 64256
Washington, DC 20029

Send us a self addressed stamped envelope and we'll send you information on how to get your profile placed on our internet site.

Other Creative Works and Projects by Lamont Carey

IMAGINE

Lamont Carey's award winning CD containing such hits as "I Can't Read", "Confidence", "I Hate This Place", "She Says

She Loves Me", and ten other electrifying spokenword pieces.

Laws Of The STREET–The Play (DVD)

Lamont Carey's playwriting directorial debut at the John F. Kennedy Center. It's a story about an inner city kid that takes the wrong path, leading to a life of murder.

Why I Keep U A Secret

A book of poems about the inner struggles and strengths of relationships told by a man who never knew love as a rose.

Learning To Be A Mommy–The Play (DVD)
Lamont Carey's second play directed at the John F. Kennedy Center. A story about a young girl who struggles while making sure her family is safe, healthy, and protected. She has to make some choices that could leave her dead and her family destroyed.

Book version forthcoming.

You're Wet
A spokenword CD by the artist known as Baby Oil. He weaves images of love and sensual appreciation on each track.

"I'm Glad You Came"
A book of poems by Baby Oil. This is pure erotica.

Upcoming projects from Lamont Carey

Capers

A story about the relationships, struggles, and inner thoughts of three teenage friends who decides to rob a kingpin drug dealer and the war that quickly ensues when his crew finds out.

The System

A fictional story about the peer pressure of one man getting released from prison and trying to change his life for the better when his buddies are getting major money in the streets.

The Redeemer

A story about the anti-Christ coming into the world as Jesus Christ.

Laws Of The STREET
The novel series & TV series

A story about a community that is forced to live under the rules set by the criminals. This is a look into the lives of those who want to escape, those who don't believe their are other options, and those who like it just the way things are.
(trailers available for viewing: www.lacareyentertainment.com)

Outside The Gate

A documentary about the struggles, strategies, and triumphs of four ex-offenders who were determined to succeed. Four different lives. Four different successes.
(Trailers available for viewing: www.lamontcarey.com)

Reach Into My Darkness. I Hate This Place

A collection of Lamont Carey's most celebrated and socially driven poems, which includes "I Can't Read", "She Says She Loves Me", "The Streets Keep Calling me", and so much more.

How to make money from spokenword
This book is a blueprint on to how to maximize your money making potential as an artist. It covers everything from protecting your material to securing performance opportunities.

Transition from prison to success
Is a self-help book about staying out of prison and living a successful life as a positive member of society

Lamont Carey is an international award-winning spokenword artist, filmmaker, playwright, actor and motivational speaker. To book Mr. Carey for worldwide speaking or performance engagements for your group, students, prisoners, employees, conferences, or at any other event you are having worldwide, contact Lamont Carey directly at:

lacareyentertainment@yahoo.com
You may visit the website at:
www.lacareyentertainment.com

Send fan mail to:

LaCarey Entertainment, LLC
P.O. Box 64256
Washington, DC 20029